JESUS: WHAT MANNER OF MAN

JESUS

What Manner of Man

Henry J. Cadbury

LONDON

S·P·C·K

1962

First published in 1947
by the Macmillan Company
First paper-back edition, 1962
S.P.C.K.
Holy Trinity Church
Marylebone Road
London N.W.1

Made and printed by offset in Great Britain by
William Clowes and Sons, Limited, London and Beccles

PREFACE

The following pages were mostly written for the Shaffer Lectures at the Yale Divinity School and were so delivered in April 1946. Parts were given as the Enoch Pond Lectures at Bangor Theological Seminary in January 1947. This accounts for their informality and contemporary references. I have attempted here to be more positive than in the *Peril of Modernizing Jesus* without myself ignoring the warning I had sounded in that volume.

The proper note with which to preface these lectures would be one of modesty. As I look back over them, I see that they are fragmentary and incomplete. Having used for titles questions asked in the gospels I would call the series "an unfinished questionnaire." The reader will notice, however, some choices in the process. Certain questions, indeed famous and urgent questions, I have scarcely touched upon at all. To many readers that may be disappointing but I have my own reasons which can be understood. Have you never started forth in your car across country and decided as far as possible to avoid the main roads and centers of population in order to see the less familiar and less travelled roads? In the same spirit I have deliberately bypassed some much debated questions of Christology and found myself by the detour on less frequented and less familiar ground.

For example, I have been more concerned with how Jesus thought than with what he thought. It is the latter that men have most wanted to know. Yet the characteristic thing about him may well have been rather the manner than the matter of his thinking. Loyalty to him as to any other teacher may well consist in following his method to independent results, rather than retaining the content of his message without conforming to the processes that gave it birth. The imitation of Christ means following his lead and that lead is not to be ascertained just by a superficial acceptance of his words. I have tried to inquire into the working of his mind, the underlying attitudes, emphases and presuppositions of his teaching, and to indicate occasionally what those same principles or methods would mean when transposed into our own life.

I have inquired into the cast of his thought. I have supposed that, whatever uncertainty besets individual sayings, any specially characteristic habits of thought and argument may still be disclosed by the general character of what remains. How he knew what he knew, and why he urged what he urged, are again not the usual questions asked of him, but they are of interest nevertheless. I have assumed that he thought of others as they should think of him, that there was a resemblance that would justify us in attributing to him what he seemed to attribute to others, and also vice versa. I have even ventured to discuss motives and aims, though I know how delicate a matter it is to probe correctly into such matters.

The Shaffer lectureship provides an opportunity that one would suppose any New Testament scholar would welcome with alacrity. Without any limitation of theological viewpoint or restriction to a special phase of the subject, the lecturer is merely invited to deal with some aspect of the historical figure of Jesus. That subject has for years filled the focus of his study. Whether occupied with the gospels or more indirectly with the other parts of the New Testament he has ever been haunted with the desire somehow to come a little closer to a knowledge of the central personality behind the early Christian movement. Apart from his personal curiosity a professional responsibility rests upon him. Students, colleagues and friends have long made it obvious to him that they expected from him, if not oracular pronouncements, at least a few positive and unevasive answers. Such questions come to him by mail in black and white. When he is asked merely what a given Greek word means, what is the most literal translation of a piece of text, whether a certain subject is mentioned in the New Testament, answers are relatively easy. But the modern layman asks more searching because more general questions and they are not to be answered by quoting a passage or so as the inspired and conclusive reply. What I suppose my contemporaries want me to give them is some impressions of Jesus of Nazareth that I have gathered in the course of long thought and reflection upon the records. They expect of me what they expect of other experts in other fields. I wonder if I can explain why I do not respond with the alacrity which they might anticipate.

Let me illustrate by another more transient experience. The invitation to give these lectures came to me in 1941 just upon my return from a brief but vivid experience of life in one of the belligerent countries across the sea. I had actually been in England in the midst of Blitzkrieg, and that before a single American uniform was in evidence, and I found that the interest and curiosity of my friends when I returned matched somewhat my own sense of adventure. But could I satisfy them? The duration of my stay and the scope of my travels were limited. What I observed did not all fit a single pattern. General questions had to be answered if at all by generalizing from a few actual experiences, and on some matters I had happened to see or hear nothing at all that was relevant. Over there I had collected impressions from many other persons. In the light of all these limitations who was I to provide a really useful and independent judgment, even about a situation so vital, so contemporary, and in a way so familiar as was the England of 1941? All I could do was to select my own topics for comment or the giving of impressions.

Beside my own sense of incompleteness of knowledge I soon found another baffling difficulty about my inquirers. They were too anxious about their questions to appraise correctly my answers. If I could not confirm their hopes, they were disappointed, even though in place of the favorable judgment that they wished for I provided an equally favorable one but different. They asked me questions that nobody could be expected to answer, least of all a transient visitor. When met by a cautious reply they went away thinking just what they wished to think, as though I had confirmed them. I found that newspaper reporters who interviewed me would make me say too little or too much and I therefore said nothing.

Now my experience with Jesus, if I may say so, is much the same. All that is recorded about him, if compressed, could have been experienced in three or four vivid weeks. On many subjects the gospels contain either no data, or little data, or divergent data. For me at least everything in the gospels is secondhand, if not more stages removed from my own eyewitness knowledge. About Jesus, too, my inquirers are often far from objective. They have preconceived ideas about him and his associates quite as much as modern Americans had about Churchill and Bevin. If my emphases do not agree with what they have thought, no matter if they are from some viewpoints more favorable, or at least better founded, they will be attentively listened to, but so far as they are assimilated they become unrecognizable in the pattern of superlatives and conventionalities which my inquirers have inherited, or themselves concocted, particularly those features they have actually preached about.

These difficulties in my hearers I am used to and I am prepared to proceed in spite of them, but I cannot ignore the difficulties inherent in myself and in the subject. That I may have prejudices too I would be the first to admit, and I ought at least to know as well as anyone the difficulties of judgment which beset any verdict concerning even simple and apparently objective matters connected with Jesus of Nazareth.

Between 1930 when the Shaffer Lectureship was founded and 1944, sixteen series of lectures on this foundation have been given at Yale but only six of the sixteen have been published. None of the lecturers were persons otherwise known to be averse to publication. Yet for reasons which one can only conjecture they apparently felt some diffidence about their accomplishment when it was over. I can sympathize with that diffidence.

H. J. C.

CONTENTS

CHAPTER I

IS NOT THIS JESUS?

The most unbiased approach in the inquiry as to a person's character is undoubtedly the attempt to let that person's words and deeds disclose himself. Too often the Bible in particular has been attacked with a set of preconceived notions and prearranged questions, and one is aware that the answers are not satisfactory or representative. One can have sympathy rather with the desire of those readers who prefer to wait and see what the evidence itself seems to volunteer. Most Biblical figures, as examined in this patient, receptive manner, do seem spontaneously to offer certain impressions of their character. These impressions are not alike for all readers and they often fall short of the kind of clarity one would wish to attain. Is there no more searching and thorough way of using our evidence?

If "we would see Jesus," we ought to let the gospels themselves disclose the answers rather than our presuppositions. The authors of the gospels were, however, only slightly interested in what we now are trying to find. The personality of Jesus was not in our sense of the term their main concern. To a limited degree he was set up as a model for men, but much less than in the days when "The Imitation of Christ," or "In His Steps" have been best sellers. For ethical instruction the evangelists rely much more on Jesus' words than on his character, and

1

they and Paul use the example of Jesus as confirmation rather than as source of ethical standards.

The gospels did not aim to describe his personality. In so far as we can find it in them we shall be reading between the lines. Some have doubted whether such an effort is legitimate or desirable and many have felt even graver doubts about the success of such a quest.

The problem of describing a person is not an unusual one. Many of us are constantly being asked, about living individuals, not dissimilar questions. As employers, pastors or teachers, or merely as acquaintances, what a variety of requests we get as "reference" for some young person who is being considered for a job. Obviously it should make a difference in our reply what sort of position is under consideration, though often the inquiries fail to indicate this. Is it irreverent to test our knowledge of Jesus by similar inquiries? I have often wondered what we should do with him occupationally in our present society. Is he more of a teacher or a preacher or a social worker? Would he fit into any department of modern life, let us say, in a university? What chair would best be offered him in a divinity school? Certainly the Old Testament rather than the New; certainly Ethics rather than Theology.

Or if we despair of classifying Jesus in terms of occupational aptitude, can we succeed any better in categories of character? There is an unusually thorough questionnaire used by one employing agency that often writes to me, which will indicate our difficulties. It contains a series of questions and provides with each question a set of graded answers that need merely be ticked off for reply. For example:

1. Impression of appearance, especially facial expression, physique, carriage.
3. Ease in meeting people.
6. Independent in thought and action without being dictatorial.
7. Interest in social problems.
10. Sense of humor.
11. Coöperation with others.
14. Sense of responsibility.
15. Adaptability to unforeseen and possibly unpleasant tasks.
17. Health.
18. Religious interest.

Imagine the difficulty in answering such a questionnaire except for persons we know quite well. The honest answer often is simply, "I do not know." I find myself guessing in accordance with my generally favorable or unfavorable view of a person without actual basis of knowledge. Many of the persons I have known for at most three years and then, apart from classroom formalities, only in a few personal conversations and casual contacts which would amount to perhaps a total of fifteen or twenty hours.

The situation would be no different if I were asked these questions about Jesus. I do not really know; for the evidence covers quite a limited collection of episodes during a very few years and does not really indicate a satisfactory basis for reply. The questionnaire makes plain what answer would be most acceptable. Thus under "Sense of Humor" one may check either "Keen," "Average," "Below Average," or "Poor." I have read various analyses of Jesus' sense of humor but they are not very convincing. Some writers credit him with a good amount, others deny him any humor at all. The temptation is to accept the modern preference for persons with such a sense and to attribute it somehow to Jesus. So in the case of "Coöperation with others." That sounds all right in a modern applicant, and obviously one would rather check either "Willing to coöperate at large sacrifice" or "Good team worker" than "Coöperates for personal gain" or "Very selfish."

I know of nothing that more clearly shows the limitations of our knowledge about Jesus than the attempt to answer for him such a recommendation blank. More than that it discloses the very special character of our contemporary standards of judgment.

Here is another form, at first sight simpler to answer. It has only five questions:

A. How are you and others affected by his appearance and manner?
B. Does he need frequent prodding, or does he go ahead without being told?
C. Does he get others to do what he wishes?
D. How does he control his emotions?
E. Has he a program with definite purpose in terms of which he distributes his time and energy?

How would you answer these questions of Jesus? I need not read you the alternative answers proposed. Perhaps the answers for Jesus would not be unanimously favorable. Some of them sound ridiculously modern and complacent in their modernness:

Displays marked ability to lead his fellows: makes things go.
Engrossed in realizing well formulated objectives.

I have already suggested elsewhere that the last qualification, "a program with a definite purpose," may not be
at all characteristic of Jesus. This form wisely provides for
each question, as one alternative, the answer, "No opportunity to observe," and in case an answer is attempted the
salutary safeguard: "Please record here instances on
which you base your judgment."

It may seem irreverent to apply to Jesus the tests that
you would use of a candidate for councillor at a boy's
camp or of an applicant for a research fellowship in chem-
istry, and yet in all our thinking of Jesus we are prone to
use modern tests of excellence of character. Behind this
lies the assumption that he was a success, that he was
highly appreciated by some persons, and that he exercised
influence, and that such a record in the First Century as in
the Twentieth involves many of the qualities which rank
well by modern judgments.

Something further should be said about the inferences
concerning Jesus drawn from the movement that followed
him. There can be no doubt that he was the central figure
in a religious movement and that that movement included some persons at least who had known him before
his death. What he had been must have had some bearing
on their loyalty to him and on their anticipation of what
he was to be. It would be a mistake, however, to judge
their loyalty by our own. The things in Jesus that impressed them need not correspond with what others would
admire. Power to work cures, for example, or to predict

the future, have no dependable correlation with moral insight or spiritual maturity. To which quality in Jesus is the Christian movement evidence? I am not suggesting that the early believers were misled or that in any sense Jesus was by their standards unworthy of their confidence. But what were their standards?

The messianic element in Jesus is a controversial subject and need not be discussed at this point in any detail. It illustrates our uncertainty as to the traits of Jesus that appealed to his followers. There is not much reason to think that messianic belief would be elicited by any of the admirable traits of character that are suggested by the questionnaires we have been following. The liberal historian has long found it necessary to explain how the Jesus that he pictures could ever have received messianic honors. The disciples were not looking for a suffering Messiah, neither were they looking for the embodiment of sweetness and light, of grace and truth as the destined Son of Man. The historian would have us believe that somehow Jesus, with his admirable though wholly unexpected qualities of inner integrity and human friendliness, supplanted the official expectation, and was substituted for the different rôle and qualifications.

Such a reading of history is rather extraordinary, and its proponents glory in its strangeness. In what high degree those moral and spiritual qualities predicated of Jesus must have existed if they were to win the attachment of friends to Jesus not merely as to a friend but as to the Anointed of God! Admirable character no doubt is always admirable and is appreciated in all ages and by all kinds of men, not merely by the wise and prudent. The historian may well ask whether it will be interpreted by

Galilean fishermen as identifying the Messiah. Surely the supernatural element in the gospels, even if unhistorical, would fit better the psychological demands of history.

Compared with the practical questionnaires for use by personnel agencies in selecting employees, there exist various more academic, perhaps more scientific, tests for classifying character. One psychologist has worked out what he calls "character clusters"; others deal with "Thematic Apperceptive Tests." Applying these to Jesus is, however, not easy, precisely because of our insufficient information about him. Every human character is somewhat inscrutable, and ancient persons have all a further element alien to ourselves. Our alienness and our ignorance of Jesus must not be accepted as proof of a divine mystery in him. An honest effort to discover in the gospel records any trait or trend of character, even on the level of the simplest human classifications, is the beginning if not the end of wisdom and ought not to be too lightly set aside. How surprising it is that in all the voluminous literature about him this approach is so rare.

We know that an artist who would paint a portrait of Jesus has no authentic data to draw on. The gospels give no hint of his stature, or his complexion, the color of his eyes or of his hair. Surely more important for us to obtain would be a profile of his mind, an insight into his approach to problems, into his habits of thought, his methods of argument, the color of his moods. Even those writers who today accept uncritically the whole contents of our four gospels appear more anxious to vindicate for him certain norms of omniscience or of messianic self-consciousness than to begin with the simpler task of seek-

ing any characteristics of mind that the records themselves disclose.

Even when writers seem to begin with unbiased inquiry and to build up a logical case for evidence, a whole
series of assumptions, of false dilemmas, and of forgotten
alternatives may occur and mislead the unwary reader.

There are certain ways of dividing mankind into opposite categories. One of these pairs used of late is ex-
trovert and introvert. To which group shall we assign
Jesus? Much of the most appreciative writing about him
runs the risk of putting him into the introvert class. Indeed, as is well known, the emphasis of orthodoxy upon
his messianic claims and messianic consciousness led some
psychiatrists to doubt his sanity. Is it evidence, or merely
prejudice, that makes some of us prefer the other reading
of his character? The apparently objective and unself-
conscious way in which he moves about in the gospel
story seems to us a perfectly natural historical portrait,
and one hesitates to add to it a deep and hidden awareness of something else. Yet precisely that is often done,
until one can write a whole book on "Christ in the
Gospels" with hardly a hint of normal human behavior.[1]

Or let us take another one of these rather superficial
psychological contrasts, that between pessimist and optimist. This question about Jesus is all the more intri-
guing because there is some evidence that in this respect
the evangelists Matthew and Luke differed in their portrait. I have quoted elsewhere [2] a series of passages in the

[1] *Christ in the Gospels,* by A. E. J. Rawlinson, 1944.
[2] *The Making of Luke-Acts,* 1927, pp. 266 f.

Sermon on the Mount where, parallel to Matthew's somewhat gloomy phrasing, a note of cheerfulness breaks through the Lucan version. I am not sure one can get behind the variant moods of the evangelists to the original temper of Jesus or even to the wording of the written source which perhaps both of them are using. There are some reasons for thinking that Luke has rather brightened the picture. Yet there is another series of passages, and precisely in the same gospel of Luke, where Jesus appears not as an optimist himself but as the dampener of other persons' enthusiasm. This includes the passages where the over-eager expectation of the second coming is met with suggestion of indefinite delay.[3] When a woman exclaims, "Blessed is the womb that bare thee and the breasts that thou didst suck," Jesus at once makes a contrary suggestion, while to another enthusiastic beatitude: "Blessed is he that shall eat bread in the kingdom of God," Jesus in Luke comes back with a somber parable of the total exclusion from the coveted meal of every one of the invited guests. It is Luke who appends at once, to the story of the triumphal entry, Jesus' prophetic lament over Jerusalem because, like a Cassandra, he saw that the doomed city had not known the things that belonged to its peace.

Are these features of Luke accidental? Are they merely artistry or literary pathos? Are they due to the evangelist's own disposition? Or was Jesus himself a kind of kill-joy, throwing cold water on other persons' enthusiasm? It is

---

[3] See *ibid.*, pp. 292 ff. Referring to the saying, "Nevertheless when the Son of man comes, will he find faith on the earth?" which follows the parable and promise that God will avenge his elect speedily, Montefiore, *Synoptic Gospels*, 1927, ii. 554 remarks: "The words seem a sort of damper upon the jubilant expectancy of the rest of the passage."

not always that way, for in the same gospel and at the same triumphal entry we read:

And some of the Pharisees from the multitude said unto him, Teacher, rebuke thy disciples. And he answered and said, I tell you, that if these shall hold their peace, the stones will cry out.

According to the gospels Jesus accused the men of his generation of being hard to please. They welcomed neither the ascetic John nor the socially tolerant Jesus. They were like children in the market place playing first wedding and then funeral but never able to agree among themselves. Were not Jesus' own comments now critical, now commendatory? Might not his hearers have accused him of perverseness, in his very own words?

We have piped unto you and you have not danced;
We have mourned unto you and you have not wept.

This incident, contrasting John and Jesus, includes a self-characterization of Jesus that has as much right to be regarded as authentic as any in the gospels, for it is a quotation by Jesus himself of the current hearsay about him. It is, to be sure, hostile and unflattering, but Jesus could hardly have quoted it if it did not represent a modicum of truth. Those who disposed of John's austerity as insanity criticized Jesus' unascetic life when he came "eating and drinking"; Jesus quotes them as calling him "a gluttonous man and a winebibber, a friend of publicans and sinners." Special interest always applies to passages like this one, where Jesus is definitely speaking of himself.

Another phrase from the gospels is declared by one writer to be the only self-description of Jesus; it is his two-fold advice to his disciples to be "wise as serpents and innocent as doves." Another writer has found autobiographical insight into Jesus' character especially in the parables of the builder of a tower and of the king about to engage in battle. They seem to him to prove that Jesus himself aimed at a definite end and chose the methods and procedure that he believed would best accomplish it.

Of course the temptation narrative is often selected as autobiographical. This is because we do not know from what other source than from Jesus himself the record of it can have been ultimately derived. What traits of character does it disclose? Independence? Fixed intentions as to ends and means? Negative reaction to the suggestions of others?

In case anyone thinks it irreverent to subject Jesus to this kind of analysis, I may remind him that even for this the gospels supply some precedent. They are full of questions asked about Jesus. Often they give no direct reply, and the questions perhaps should be understood in the original as merely rhetorical, or even as exclamations of admiration or hostility:

"Who is this?" "What sort of person is this?" "What is this—a new teaching?" "Whence did this fellow get this wisdom?" "Why does this man welcome sinners?" "By what authority do you do this?" "Why do you speak in parables?" "Why does he speak this way?" "Why does he eat with publicans and sinners?" "How has this man known without having studied?" "Have any of the rulers believed in him?" "How do you think?" "What do you say about yourself?"

Much that I intend to ask hereafter is reminiscent of some of these questions in the gospels.

One of the leading questions with which it is legitimate to begin is the very general inquiry as to what were Jesus' own interests. Before assailing the records of him with special interests of our own, we may fairly ask what were his own concerns. To judge from the gospels, what was the center of his attention? This is a merely statistical or quantitative inquiry.

The synoptic gospels answer this question rather easily. Jesus had a good deal to say about human conduct, about man's behavior to his fellows. The Fourth Gospel by its emphasis on Christology in the words of Jesus brings this ethical element in the other gospels into strong relief. Those who rate the historical accuracy of the Three above the Fourth accept the impression of Jesus' concern for morals as a true impression. This emphasis can easily be fitted into other features of history. It agrees, we know from a study of contemporary life, with some Jewish emphases of the period. The questions Jesus considered were being considered by the rabbis of his time. No doubt Hillel, John the Baptist, Gamaliel and Akiba had occasion to speak about covetousness, lust, anger, revenge, censoriousness and other like subjects. To know that topics like these were in the air confirms as accurate the impression given by the gospels that Jesus also was concerned with them.

A central interest in ethics is compatible with the outward circumstances of Jesus' life. He seems to have been a private and public advisor of men. Perhaps personal counselling played an even larger part than our gospels

indicate. I think in the sermons in Matthew and elsewhere individual remarks of Jesus have been generalized
in audience and in application. The gospels still contain
plenty of evidence that Jesus' words were the response
to specific occasions. Different individuals who encountered him presented different problems. The answer usually had to do neither with theological belief nor with
public policy, but with personal behavior.

The circumstances of Jesus' death are not incompati-
ble with this mainly ethical interest. The Jewish authorities accused him of blasphemy and the Romans accused
him of treason. Accusers rarely sense the real interests
of their victims. Socrates was accused of bringing in new
gods. Socrates, too, I take it, was an ethical teacher. Even
today men see religious heresy or political treason in
radical morality.

Even the apocalyptic element in the gospels and whatever of Christological thought should be traced back to
Jesus himself are consonant with an ethical emphasis on
his part. The framework of an expected day of judgment
would be part of the current outlook on the future,
shared alike by Jesus and his hearers, and would be a
natural setting and an effective sanction for every ethical
judgment. The concern of Jesus was not so much why
one should be moral as what one's moral duty is. Jesus'
teaching indicates whatever old or new, common or individual opinion, he held upon this subject. An apocalyptic
outlook might sharpen the sense of urgency; it need not
greatly affect the character of the moral judgments.

Perhaps I should underscore this point a little further.
Too often it is assumed that the apocalyptic outlook of
the gospels affected the content of the ethics. Logically

perhaps it should have done so, but practically I believe that was not the case. Moral verdicts of individuals are based on other factors than the calculation of the proximity of the end. The ethic of Jesus is not an interim ethic; neither is it the ethic for a utopia. The vivid hope of a utopia and the feeling of living in the interim may make men more concerned to be faithful to God's moral will for them. Jesus used that leverage to the utmost. That perspective and leverage do not reveal the nature and sources of Jesus' ethical judgments. After all, a long and rich ethical tradition stretches behind him, especially in the prophets, and personal experience and moral insight are a natural source of any individual opinions.

Is there any reason to assign to the evangelists rather than to Jesus this ethical interest? Is this a case where later emphases have overshadowed the historical facts and have altered the perspective? Certainly the trend of the Christian movement which we have been taught to look for was much more theological than practical. In fact, the synoptic gospels have seemed to many to be a phenomenon difficult to place in the history of the church, precisely because of their specially ethical interest, and it would be still more difficult to suppose that the church invented them. Was there a Christianity in those early days more concerned with standards of conduct than Jesus was? If so, we shall have to take with caution the apparent centrality of ethics in the gospels. Perhaps the contrast is not so great, nor theology and ethics so mutually exclusive. The unknown channels through which the synoptic tradition has come down to us may have included a strong practical interest in conduct which has selected, not to say exaggerated, such ethical precepts as belonged to the original memories of Jesus. I am, however, inclined to believe that the emphasis was there from the beginning.

If we accept this ethical element as genuine to Jesus, can we by the same clue of general proportion find within the extant ethical teaching any prevailing motif or characteristic? Are there any kinds of virtues or vices which secure repeated attention? Now I do not intend to sketch the whole variety of ethical phases or interests which could, one by one, be tested by our gospel material. One observation arises from the most superficial recollection of the contents of these records. It is this: that a large place is held by the renunciatory type of injunctions. To judge again merely from the proportion within the remaining material, Jesus repeatedly pressed upon his hearers that attitude which does not push one's own desires, interests, rights or advantages. Giving and forgiving, humility and submission, self-restraint and self-denial occupy an important proportion of the sayings. To put it negatively—and Jesus does not share the modern aversion to negatives and prohibitions—he was advising his hearers not to condemn others, not to resist, not to revenge, not to be ambitious for themselves, not to exalt themselves. Judged simply quantitatively this renunciatory ethical emphasis seems to emerge from the gospels.

Such simple ways of getting at the central characteristics of Jesus are not very satisfactory. Self-renunciation can be of very varying kinds and for very varying motives and its negative character may be merely a resultant from a much more positive central control. Yet it is worth while to remind ourselves of what is really articulate in the gospels,—the cost of discipleship. Jesus' teaching of non-resistance, a subject so controversial in the context of our present world, is only a part of the most characteristic aspect of the gospels.

Again we ask, however, whether this emphasis may not be due more to his reporters than to Jesus himself. Possibly they, more than he, felt the burdens of discipleship. His own experience and theirs could have made prominent in their thinking what men must suffer or forego. Did Jesus himself say that men must take up the cross and follow him, or has that word slipped into the records after Calvary? Was the negative aspect of Christian virtue not a deduction from experience, and perhaps the making a virtue out of a necessity? Could not a movement that came to interpret theologically to its own satisfaction the death of the Messiah, *ex post facto* also come to accept ethically the standards of the beatitudes and the cross?

I have already spoken of the fact that the same ethics may root from different causes. The self-denial inculcated in the gospels must be further examined. It may be purely ascetic, for the discipline of the denier of self. It may be primarily altruistic, for the benefit of others. Or it may be merely fatalistic, or at least the necessary concomitant of membership in a persecuted and unpopular group. The last seems to me the true answer for much of the gospel material. Neither the ascetic nor the altruistic motive is the real center of this teaching. I will not deny the possibility of an asceticism of a sort. We know now that asceticism is not entirely foreign to First Century Judaism, and there are features of eschatology which would further voluntary self-denial. So long as it was thought that the future would provide recompense for the present, evil in this life was worth bearing or even seeking, for the sake of the opposite in the world to come. Indeed, our distress, even voluntary distress, might induce God to hasten the days of the Messiah, by arousing the divine pity.

Voluntary discipline is not the only condition of fortitude. Many of the passages in the gospels inculcating the virtues of which we are speaking contemplate neither nature nor the supernatural as causing men trouble, but human ill-will and persecution. The historical reasons for the prominence of this idea are well known to us in the early church. Paul is witness not only for himself and his churches, but also for the Jewish Christians, that they had to meet hostility from men. We must, therefore, leave the possibility open that some of these more somber aspects of the gospel ethic are due to the medium through which the material passed rather than to Jesus himself. In Mark especially it has been thought that both the presentation of Jesus' life and some of his sayings have been influenced by a kind of martyr motive.

Chapter II

WHENCE THIS WISDOM?

No matter how oracular the teaching of Jesus seems to be, it may well be searched for any favorite form of argument. Some would claim that for himself the truths he uttered were "given to him" without need of supporting logic, and that the reasons he adduces, no matter how simple and self-evident, were adopted by him for purely pedagogical purposes. Even so, any analysis of these reasons will throw light on the minds of his contemporaries and followers, and they may be characteristic even of his own mental processes.

Familiar in the gospels and in the contemporary Judaism as well is the *a fortiori* argument—the "light and heavy," as the rabbis called it:

If God so clothe the grass . . . shall he not much more clothe you?

If ye being evil know how to give good gifts to your children, how much more shall your Father which is in heaven?

Or in less explicit form:

Not a sparrow falls to the ground . . . you are of more value than many sparrows.

Behold the birds of the heaven . . . your heavenly Father feeds them . . . Are not you of much more value than they?

18

If they do this in the green tree what shall be done in the
dry?

Which of you by being anxious can add a cubit to your span
of life? If then you are not able to do that which is least,
why are you anxious about the rest?

What man of you does not rescue on the sabbath day a do-
mestic animal that has fallen into a well, or does not
even merely lead it to water? How much then is a man
of more value than a sheep?

Another type of argument is drawn from simple considerations of equivalence:

The measure you give is the measure you get.

Freely you have received, freely give.

If you forgive not men their trespasses neither will your
heavenly Father forgive you.

He that receives you receives me, and he that receives me
receives him that sent me.

Or indirectly,

Which is easier to say "Thy sins are forgiven," or to say
"Arise and take up thy bed and walk?"

It is in this form of comparison that Old Testament
examples often occur on the lips of Jesus. If the disciples'
plucking of grain on the sabbath is illegal, what about
David's eating of the shewbread? If the wicked contemporaries of Noah and Lot were unheedful of the coming
cataclysms of flood or fire, so shall be the heedless generation when the Son of Man comes.

In other instances parallelism and *a fortiori* are combined, as when the repentance of the Ninevites or the respect of the Queen of Sheba is cited with comment that in the ministry of Jesus something greater than Jonah or Solomon is here. Jesus' breach of the sabbath is not only parallel with the legalized priestly breach of it in the temple: it is more justifiable since something greater than the temple is here.

The familiarity of these passages and indeed their naturalness should not prevent us from recognizing in them what for lack of a better term I can only call a kind of mathematical logic. They show in Jesus' mind, if they are genuine, a kind of quantitative mentality—a tendency to deal with moral truth in terms of measure or size.

Even when Jesus follows an opposite tack and speaks in the form of paradox the quantitative element often remains:

He that is least in the kingdom of heaven is greater than John.

He that is greatest among you shall be your servant.

Whosoever shall break one of these least commandments and shall teach men so shall be called least in the kingdom of heaven.

One recognizes in this connection his fondness for proverbial superlatives of smallness—jot, tittle, mote, gnat, mustard seed, needle's eye; and of largeness—beam, camel, sycamine tree, mountain. The terms chosen are unoriginal and conventional, but they are expressive, and in the recorded sayings of Jesus they are relatively numerous. They again suggest a quantitative type of thinking.

Possibly Jesus' whole use of parables should be connected with this habit of mind. Parables also, we now know, were thoroughly characteristic of the same rabbis whom we find so fond of the *a fortiori* argument. They are argument by analogy. In many cases Jesus seems to combine the two processes. He argues from human behavior and from the processes of nature to spiritual truths. He does not hesitate to infer that what man does God also will do, or will be even more likely to do. A churlish parent does not answer a son's petition for bread or fish by offering useless objects. A lazy neighbor and an unjust judge ultimately respond to importunity. A shepherd seeks a lost sheep with energy even when ninety-nine others are perfectly safe. How much more will God care for the requests and needs of his human children!

The figurative language of Jesus—parable, simile, metaphor—is extraordinarily pervasive in our gospels. To judge from these remains Mark is not far wrong when he says, "Without a parable spake he not unto them." One can easily set this down to the figurative or poetical character of his mind, or to the pedagogical purpose which skilfully selected this method of teaching as most effective. One may attribute the abundance of parables to a natural selectiveness in the memory of his first hearers. I would like to suggest that it goes even deeper than that. Possibly Jesus himself regularly thought in such terms. Whether by induction or by illustration, spiritual truth came to him in close association with the observable data of outward life. He assumed a kind of mathematical consistency between the natural world and the spiritual, a consistency so taken for granted that he was scarcely aware of making the transition. His teaching merely called his hearers' attention to the application or extension of acknowledged tangible data. "From the fig tree learn its parable," he said, and he expected his hearers to do the same with all trees, with all nature and with the social life of men. It is evident, for example, that a kingdom divided against itself cannot stand. It must be equally evident that demons are not cast out by Beelzebub. It is evident that one does not gather figs of thistles. So clearly an evil man cannot produce good fruit.

It has been said of a well-known astrophysicist, the late Sir Arthur S. Eddington, that he was a great believer in analogy.

This strong awareness of analogy is the secret of all great imaginative penetration. The perception of unities among things that are different is the foundation of truth. The leap of a scientist to a hypothesis, no less than the images with which the poet or inspired teacher exhibits the underlying unity of complex manifestations is a creative cognition inexplicable by any mechanical description of the laws of thought—the fundamental experience of which the describable 'processes' of thought are an elaboration. All human analogies break down because they represent only parts of the truth, but the inspired souls whose vision has lighted our path are right nevertheless in clinging to analogy as yielding fragments that have their own validity and, if used with scrupulous discrimination, accepted often as suggestion rather than firm and detailed truth, can be built at last into an abiding whole.[1]

[1] Reginald A. Smith, "The Religious Significance of Eddington," *The Modern Churchman*, xxxiv, 1944–45, p. 335 f.

Something of the same sort of mathematical habit seems characteristic of the mind of Christ. Was there not then a pre-scientific assumption of consistency, a readiness to leap from the experience without to the experience within? Many of Eddington's fellow scientists were rather critical of his unverified religious beliefs. Probably the method of Jesus will not commend itself to the wise and prudent of our day any more than to those of his day. Our concern is not to commend but to discover if possible how his mind was wont to work.

Only slightly less simple than the kinds of argument considered is the principle of what I may call proportionate duty. It is well expressed in the saying:

To whomsoever much is given, of him shall much be required;
And to whom they commit much, of him will they ask the more.

Its importance in the thinking of Jesus does not depend on a single text, and its significance in the modern world is far from accepted. We are of course familiar with graded or graduated duties as well as with even or equal requirements. The income tax is an example of the principle of proportion, while the poll tax represents a flat assessment alike for all persons. In athletics also we have the ordinary contest in which all contestants begin from scratch, but there is also the handicap system which attempts to demand higher achievement from those who enter with known higher qualifications.

One of the characteristics of law, whether Mosaic or modern, is its tendency to require of all persons a flat minimum. Though concessions are sometimes made to minors or other classes, the ordinary law prohibits to all alike certain acts and tacitly sanctions what it does not forbid. Anyone who drives a car at all, may drive up to the speed limit, and none, no matter how expert, is supposed to travel faster. But morality as distinct from law can suggest variation of duty between individuals proportionate to their several privileges, and even penology is at long last beginning to recognize this principle and its conflict with absolute law.

Now some sayings of Jesus are so far from this principle that they seem to us almost wilfully perverse, or at least paradoxical. For example:

To him that has shall be given,
And from him that has not shall be taken even what he has.

This sentiment evidently offended some early Christians as nonsense for it was modified by substituting at the end the words "what he seems to have." In the parable of the laborers hired successively to work out the day in a vineyard, instead of payment proportionate to hours of labor, Jesus represents the employer as giving "unto this last" even as unto those who had "borne the burden and the heat of the day." Ruskin was not the first reader of the gospels to be struck by this passage.

The other principle appeals to us as both reasonable and just. It has a logical validity. "To whomsoever much is given, of him shall much be required; and to whom they commit much, of him they will ask the more." To each according to his need, and from each according to his opportunity. Were we to press the wording of the second line of the couplet, "To whom *much* is committed of him will *more* be required"—we might find something even more exacting than proportionate responsibility from the highly privileged. We might assume a kind of surtax in the moral realm that goes up more steeply than on a scale of exact proportion.

Jesus' application of this principle is rather pervasive in the gospels. It shows particularly in his attitude to the privileged groups to whom he spoke. For in spite of his words, "I came not to call the righteous but sinners to repentance," Jesus seems to have had a great deal to say to the righteous or self-righteous among his people. His sympathy for the dispossessed or underprivileged persons or for the exploited groups need not be questioned. Yet many of his remarks are (or originally were) addressed to the favored persons. The rich are shamed by the poor widow's two mites, Simon the Pharisee is shamed for his social neglect by the sinful woman's improvised ministrations with her tears and her hair. Even the well-behaved older son is less the hero than the truly penitent prodigal. The priest and Levite are eclipsed by a mere Samaritan. The Jews for all their privileges will find themselves cast out while many will come from the East and the West, from the North and the South, and recline at the messianic banquet. Others than the first chosen guests will eat the meal. More faithful servants will be found for the Lord's vineyard than the normal tenants.

There is reason to believe that it is not so much the pretensions of the Pharisees that Jesus criticizes as their failure to live up to their own standards or to yield fruits proportionate to their sometimes well justified feeling of advantage. He requires no less than they did, but rather more—a righteousness that exceeds the righteous-

ness of the scribes and Pharisees. Even on the level of
equality the publicans and harlots are justified rather
than the Pharisees in their response to John the Baptist.
From praying in the temple a publican goes down justified rather than does the Pharisee, but not because the
publican is not a sinner, or the Pharisee not in many
ways exemplary.

Jesus brings home often the special privileges of his
generation. They were seeing and hearing what righteous men and kings had long desired to see. Their less
favored predecessors, even the wicked people of Sodom,
Tyre and Sidon, would, therefore, find it more tolerable
in the day of judgment than would those who rejected
Jesus' message. The Ninevites and the Queen of the South
were historic witnesses against those who ignored the
more impressive present phenomenon.

Not merely in terms of apocalyptic reversal are we to
understand the beatitudes and the woes of Jesus. In proportion to their advantages the rich have so acted as to
deserve no blessing, while the poor have often deserved
better than might have been expected of them. So the
Jew as contrasted with Samaritan or Gentile. Jesus' principle here merely echoes the stern words of the Lord in
the book of Amos to the whole family that he had brought
up out of the land of Egypt and led forty years in the
wilderness to possess the land of the Amorite.

You only have I known of all the families of the earth,
Therefore I will visit upon you all your iniquities.

What this would mean when applied to modern nations like our own is rarely recognized. Our moral condemnation of other peoples too often assumes that they

are to be judged by identical standards and if we are more decent than they, all is well with us. But if we should begin with Jesus' principle of proportionate responsibility, we would recognize that it requires of a more highly favored people not slight moral superiority, but a really great difference. Our geographical remoteness from the friction centers of Europe and Asia, our great natural resources, our abundant Lebensraum, our educational standards, our long political experience with democratic institutions and our knowledge, if not our practice, of Christian ethical standards, put on us the duty of corresponding generosity, chivalry, understanding. They make it shameful for us to imitate, even when others have started them, the military and political crimes which we so readily condemn in others and condone in ourselves. Indeed, we may realize that our sins, though perhaps only sins of omission, are less pardonable in us than the ruthless aggression and atrocities of harassed and impoverished peoples under the influence of demagogues' dictation and propaganda.

The same is true of the individual. Of a favored person is required not the general minimum, but something more. There is no beatitude pronounced upon being at least as good as others, or merely free of others' faults. It is not Jesus but the Pharisee that thanks God that he is not as other men are. How often, like the rich young ruler in the gospels, a young man comes across our path aware of the advantages that he has received of economic security and good health, of breeding and education, of family and friendships, and aware also that something more is required of him? Here is a burden he cannot today unload by getting rid of what he possesses. He can only be satisfied by a character and service to others proportionate to the advantages he has enjoyed. Nothing less will meet the moral demands he makes upon himself than a kind of voluntary overtime.

Ye have heard that it was said, An eye for an eye, and a tooth for a tooth; but I say unto you, Resist not him that is evil: but whosoever smiteth thee on thy right cheek, turn to him the other also. And if any man would go to law with thee, and take away thy coat, let him have thy cloak also. And whosoever shall compel thee to go one mile, go with him two.

As has been said by a Jewish scholar, "Jesus teaches an excess in virtue, an excess in forbearance, an excess in gentleness, an excess in giving and yielding. He *does*—and here there *is* originality—very often oppose the principle of measure for measure, and it is against this principle that he is speaking here. Virtue, the full virtue of a disciple, is an excess, a full devotion, an overflowing measure; even Aristotle, who laid down the doctrine of virtue being a mean, had also to point out that this very mean is itself, in some sense, an excess." [2]

The difficulty of finding an appropriate word for this excess, as Montefiore calls it, comes out in the following passage. In Luke it runs:

Love your enemies, do good to them that hate you, bless them that curse you, pray for them that despitefully use you. . . . And if ye love them that love you, what thank have ye? For even sinners love those that love them. And if

[2] C. G. Montefiore, *Rabbinic Literature and Gospel Teachings*, Macmillan & Co., Ltd., 1930, p. 52.

ye do good to them that do good to you, what thank have ye? for even sinners do the same. And if ye lend to them of whom ye hope to receive what thank have ye? even sinners lend to sinners to receive again as much. But love your enemies, and do them good, and lend never despairing.

In Matthew the concluding section has this parallel:

For if ye love them that love you, what reward have ye? Do not even the publicans the same? And if ye salute your brethren only, what do ye more? Do not even the Gentiles the same?

The evangelists have struggled with the terms for ordinary or unesteemed folk. Hence the variation "sinners" in Luke, and in Matthew "publicans" and "Gentiles." They have also struggled with the term for the excess. Luke's χάρις (three times) is one effort. Rather than thank (AV) or thanks it means in modern English something more like grace or favor or perhaps merit or credit. Matthew once uses μισθός (wages, hire, reward) and once a word that can mean out of the common but that is also the exact Greek for Montefiore's excess or surplus (περισσόν). Justin Martyr paraphrases by the term novelty: "What new thing do you do?" But in the light of our whole mathematical approach perhaps Matthew's simple "What do ye more?" is sufficient. That is the question asked the follower of Jesus.

C. F. Andrews in his posthumous essay on *The Sermon on the Mount* [3] tells how, in reading the Greek testament as an undergraduate at Cambridge, he had found this saying, "What do ye to excess?" and had copied it out

[3] (1942) pp. 134–136.

for himself in Greek as a question to put before himself
every day and how this motto had helped not only himself, but also, as he found out much later, a young Indian
student whom he was tutoring at that time.

There are many questions which this principle and the
context in which the gospels use it may seem to ignore.
The effect of such uncalculating generosity on the evil
doer is not cited, though a later writer makes the utilitarian revision: "Love them that hate you, then you will have
no enemy."[4] Nor is the underprivileged himself in view,
and the temptation the law of proportionate duty might
present him of doing less than the decent requirement.
The principle, as Jesus enunciates it, is simple and direct
—it is a demand for a surplus. The differentia of the
Christian is the extra, that is the extra-ordinary. We may
say that the sign of Christianity is a plus sign. Sometimes
when I see the familiar Christian symbol of the cross
my fancy simplifies all the historical and theological suggestions of which it is reminiscent into the familiar arithmetical symbol which it often resembles. *In hoc signo
vinces*—in this sign you will prevail.

There is perpetual refreshment to the Christian spirit
in this reminder of the teaching of Jesus. It has been
called by a well-known American preacher the principle
of the second mile or of unenforceable obligations. If we
try to inculcate only enforceable rules we cannot live up
even to them. It is necessary to aim at more if we would
achieve even the minimum. Coventry Patmore said,
"The way to be good, in fact the only way to be good, is
to be heroically good." When men insist that the hard
sayings of Jesus are not rules to be obeyed, not a code of

---

[4] *Didache* 1.3.

laws, they are quite right, yet that does not make our task easier but harder. For Christianity is something more.

One wonders whether Jesus ever thought of this standard as applied to himself. There are hints of it in the gospels. Even the Son of Man came not to be ministered unto but to minister and to give his life a ransom for many. Did Jesus feel a responsibility proportionate to his position? Did he correspondingly exact the extra from himself? Of course in order to answer that question one would first have to ask, How did he rate himself? But Paul, who holds a high estimate of Jesus, suggests in one famous passage that there was a deliberate connection between existing in the form of God, being equal to God, and emptying himself, humbling himself, and becoming obedient to death on a cross.

Chapter III

WHY SPEAKEST THOU IN PARABLES?

Any study of the mind of Christ must take into account his parables—a familiar and extensive part of our oldest gospels. Yet the student will be aware that this evidence is abused more easily and more often than any other. Minor details in the parables are picked upon without regard to context, and are twisted into wished-for meanings. The interpretation of Jesus' parables requires a cautious method. Fortunately the whole matter has been carefully studied in recent decades, and since Jülicher's important volumes certain legitimate principles have been worked out which the conscientious student can use if he wishes.

Following the "quantitative" test, we approach this interesting body of material in a more wholesale way than by the detailed exegesis of these several illustrations used by Jesus. Admitting that each genuine parable of his was intended by him for a special lesson and was spoken *ad hoc* for dealing with a single situation, we ask whether any conclusion can be drawn from his general practice or from the recurrent features in the parables.

In such an approach we have at least a venerable precedent. The gospels themselves comment upon Jesus as a teacher in parables. Unfortunately, in Greek, perhaps

also in Aramaic, the word applied to these illustrations
had connotations of obscurity and not of clarity. At any
rate the evangelists regard them in that light. Mark sets
the style by having Jesus explicitly declare that for those
outside, in contrast to the disciples, all things are in parables, in order that seeing they may see and not perceive
and hearing they may hear and not understand lest they
should turn and be forgiven, and he adds:

And with many such parables he spoke the word to them as
they were able to hear, and without a parable he did not
speak to them, but privately to his own disciples he explained
everything.

Matthew and Luke are not quite so emphatic on the in-
tention of obscurity, though they acknowledge obscurity as the fact or the result. Matthew after his manner
explicitly quotes the prophecy of Isaiah (6:9 f) beside
echoing its language as in the parallels, and he adds:

I will open my mouth in parables,
I will utter things hidden from the foundation of the world.

In spite of the last line, the evangelists' theory is that
parables, somewhat like Old Testament prophecy itself,
were not intended to disclose hidden truth to their first
and widest body of hearers. But this theory is partly be-
lied by their practice which is to relate the parables fully,
rarely to add explanations, and even to state at times
that the original hearers understood the purport or application of the illustration.

The modern admirers of Jesus also generally draw a
conclusion opposite to the evangelists' theory. They

charge Mark with reading into his materials a rather perverse editorial fiction, a fiction that fits his larger schemes of a messianic secret and of an inner and outer ring of Jesus' hearers; witness for the former the injunctions of silence about cures and other supernatural matters, and for the latter the repeated private explanations which follow his public utterances. The modern admirer is impressed with the parable as a literary form almost unique in the literature he knows. He recognizes its pedagogic value and he therefore finds in it a general mark of Jesus' educational skill. If better informed, he would have to acknowledge that the parables are precisely characteristic of contemporary Judaism and, so far from being an evidence of Jesus' originality, they are rather typical of his Jewishness in method and manner.[1] But since that seems to serve another apologetic purpose—the fidelity of the gospels to their local setting—he will be content to substitute one edifying conclusion for another.

If then we are to find in Jesus' parables something more distinctive of him, we must study them in comparison with those of his time. It is easy enough to claim that they are better, more vivid, less academic than those of the rabbis; but it is not so easy to vindicate such claims as free from the bias of our greater familiarity with them and from purely subjective judgment. If the gospel parables contain comparatively picturesque features it may

---

[1] As a student of literature, if not specially of the gospels, John Erskine should have known better than to say: "There is nothing in literature quite like the parables of Jesus. He created the form, and though attempts are made to imitate him, the form remains his alone" (*The Human Life of Jesus*, 1945, p. 105) or: "Literature furnishes no close parallels and no rivals to these perfect compositions. They can be explained by no study of previous authors" (*ibid.*, p. 129).

well be due to the transmission to which they have been subject, or rather to the somewhat prosy pruning which the transmitters of rabbinic material have given the parables of the rabbis. Allowing for subsequent modification in the oral tradition on each side, but in opposite directions, we may conclude that the exempla of Jesus and the rabbis may have resembled each other much more closely at first than they do now in Gospel and Talmud. The picturesque items in the gospel parables—the birds picking seed from the foot paths or roosting in the mustard trees, the fatted calf, the sheep on the shepherd's shoulder, the dogs that lick the beggar's sores, the distraught woman sweeping with her broom, the servant with his coin in a handkerchief, the highways and hedges, the innkeeper's bill, are exactly the sort of items which some kinds of transmission as well as some kinds of storytellers do not foster. The copies of gospel parables already show this pruning tendency at work, and we should simply rejoice that in the Christian records so often the picturesque and irrelevant remains. Perhaps in some cases the transmission has added such features. Luke, to judge from his narratives, could even improve his materials with vivid touches. Something like the spirit of Greek drama may have affected the parable of the Prodigal Son. We shall do well not to claim for Jesus as teacher either a unique or a superior parable technique.

A favorite comment is that at least the sources of the illustrations show the interests and attention of Jesus. It is pointed out that Paul's figures come from the city and Jesus' from the country—and this is said to the disadvantage of Paul since God made the country but man made the town. It is even inferred that Jesus had a love of nature—the birds and the lilies—and that he haunted the hills to look from nature up to nature's God. In the case of Paul the illustrations, even when urban, do not seem to me especially autobiographical. The contemporary popular preachers whom his style resembles also used illustrations but neither he nor they seem to use them very freshly. The figure of the body and its members is traditional. The athlete, the builder and the farmer —for even Paul knows planting and watering—are conventional. He is sometimes ridiculed for his statement that the law against muzzling the ox shows God's interest in preachers and not in oxen. Note that it is an agricultural illustration but that it comes out of a book. Certainly Jesus' ideas are not bookish, though he too uses scripture, as David's eating shewbread and events connected with Abel, Lot, Solomon, Elijah, Elisha, or Jonah. Even his illustration of the care of oxen—the care of them on the sabbath—we know was a moot point of contemporary scribal controversy. It is really going too far to suppose that everything Jesus said was based upon a personal experience—whether of an ox languishing on the sabbath or of a wounded victim of highwaymen, or of a neighbor's importunity at midnight, or of bridesmaids excluded from a wedding.

As for a love of nature I must refer you to the studies in the history of ideas—a science which may provide an increasing amount of assistance in checking on the mind of Christ. The love of nature, in the sense in which it has been felt since the romantic movement, appears to have been absent from the ancient world. This may be hard for us to believe, but it is probably true, and we had better accept it and prepare ourselves to meet things still harder to believe.

Perhaps more of Jesus' interests is to be seen in the subjects he illustrates than in the sources of his illustrations. Unfortunately we do not always know the subject. The evangelists sometimes repeat the parable without saying what it illustrates and we find ourselves in the position of the modern minister whose enthusiastic parishioner offered him what she thought an extremely useful illustration but, when asked what it would illustrate, said she did not know, she was leaving that to him. Even when the evangelists do give their ideas of what Jesus was using the parable for, we have not always confidence in their application. Luke somewhat regularly provides a setting: "He told a parable [on humility] to those who were invited when he noted how they chose out the chief seats" (14:7). The parable of the lost sheep with others is assigned by Luke to an occasion when the Pharisees and scribes murmured about Jesus' friendliness to sinners (15:1, 2). He told the parable of the pounds "because he was near Jerusalem and they supposed that the kingdom of God would appear immediately" (19:11). We are not very happily situated when we are compelled to rely for our understanding of the parables on such editorial explanations, or on the gospel context, or on the mere content of the parable itself.

We are not carried much forward by the assumption that many if not all the parables deal with the kingdom of God. The basis for that view seems authoritative enough. Mark's parable of the seed growing secretly and the twin parables of the mustard seed and of leaven representing both our oldest sources, Mark and Q (if I may use the current theory of gospel origins), begin with the question or statement of what the kingdom of God is like. Matthew, who here and elsewhere substitutes the synonymous "kingdom of Heaven," has four more parables in the same chapter beginning the same way, beside four others elsewhere (18:23; 20:1; 22:2; 25:1), not to mention his free use of the word "kingdom" in parables or in their explanations. "The kingdom of Heaven is like (or likened) unto" is plainly a formula of a writer much given to formulas.

Now there is no denying the currency of the phrase, kingdom of God, in all our gospel sources. Entirely apart from the parables, that term would play an important part in any study of the terminology of Jesus. Almost everything that Jesus said can be associated with the kingdom. But I must express my feeling that a term like that was so conventional and so inclusive that it would be a mistake to expect to find the key to Jesus' interests by our own attempt to narrow the term down to some special implication of the term, whether etymological or exegetical. We are, as a matter of fact, presented with rival interpretations of the term. Some would stress the sovereignty of God implicit in it—a theistic note, while others, especially in connection with the slogans of certain belligerents in World Wars I and II, are impressed with its democratic implications rather than with its royal authoritarianism. That it involves a group of persons and their relationships seems to other interpreters to give it social significance. There is also of course much reason to regard the term as temporal like our

English noun "reign" and to connect it with an apocalyptic program of the future.

Whatever be its most probable or prevalent meaning,
it provides in the parables no centralizing subject, but
rather a convenient way of doing what we do when we
say: "Life is like this," "Truth or duty may be illustrated by this," "Here is the way it seems to me." The
so-called parables of the kingdom are no special
portion of Jesus' teaching. They are no more limited to
the kingdom than those without that phrase.

I am surprised that we do not hear more of another
feature of the parables, and I think a less superficial one,
their use of the biological feature of growth. No doubt
earlier generations were much more interested in religion as miracle or divine fiat or as sudden unprepared
conversion than in any psychology of religion which resembled the slow evolutionary processes of nature. Mark's
parable of the seed growing secretly seems to stress the
element of progress by stages, the automatic character
of change, and its unobserved if not unobservable pro-
gression. When one adds the parables of the mustard
seed, of the sower, of the wheat and the tares, of the
fruitless fig tree, of the rich fool with his full barns, and
three parables of vineyards or vineyard workers (Matt.
20:1-16; 21:28-32; Mark 12:1-12 and parallels), not to
mention the less obviously biological parable of the
leaven, we seem to get in the parables a rather important
recurrence of the element of growth and fruition.

Perhaps one can go even further and say that a special
attitude towards the future is indicated by more than

one of these illustrations from vegetable growth. Not all of them are intended to excite the hope of the future. They teach men to be patient with delay because, like the sequence of nature, the future cannot be hurried and men will have to wait for it. The parable of the seed growing secretly is perhaps better called the parable of the patient farmer. "If the several stages in the growth of the crop are enumerated, 'first the blade, then the ear, then the full corn in the ear,' that is not in order to suggest the idea of slow development, but of an appointed order which may not be hurried or deranged."[2] Matthew's parable of the tares, even if secondary and in part dependent on the one just mentioned, recommends waiting instead of trying to sort out prematurely the weeds from the wheat. While the parable of the fig tree is defined in one case as teaching that her tender branch and budding leaves are harbingers of summer, the parable of the unfruitful fig tree is another case of the recommendation for further delay, before drastic action is taken. Long after Jesus' time Christians were using the processes of nature to teach the same lesson. "Be patient therefore," says the Epistle of James, "until the coming of the Lord. Behold the husbandman waiteth for the precious fruit of the earth, being patient over it, until it receive the early and latter rain. Be ye also patient: establish your hearts." And a lost scripture, possibly of still earlier date, but known to us only in later quotation, reminds the reader of the sequence of nature as a ground for ultimate certainty as well as for present patience.

[2] B. D. T. Smith, *The Parables of the Synoptic Gospels*, 1937, p. 130. Cf. R. Bultmann, *Jesus and the Word*, p. 36.

O you fools, consider a plant, a grapevine for example.
First it sheds the old leaves, then the young shoots sprout,
then leaves, then flowers, then the green grapes, finally the
ripe grapes appear. You see how quickly the fruit is ripe.
Even so quickly and suddenly will God's final judgment
come. (1 Clem. 23.4; 2 Clem. 11.3)

Certainly for the apostolic age the anticipation of the
Lord's coming required some delicate adjustment between a too eager and a too hopeless attitude. Both
Paul's letters to Thessalonica deal apparently with problems that arose because his converts were not ready for
the actual delay. The gospels too (especially Luke), for
all their insistence on God's sure and final act, have
plenty of warning against pre-dating the end. They remind us again and again, like Paul, that certain other
things must happen first, and that there is no way for us to
shorten or to avoid the waiting and endurance which the
interim demands of men. Obviously some early Christians
had over-advertized this hope. Appropriate as all this is
after Jesus' day, I am not sure it was not appropriate to
some features in his own time. It may represent a problem
of his own life and thought. "Hope deferred maketh the
heart sick." John the Baptist preached the near coming
of the kingdom of God, and Jesus heard him. John was
not sure whether Jesus was its harbinger or whether to
look for someone else. From John's day on men were
attempting to take the kingdom by storm. To Jesus were
addressed the impatient questions, "When? How soon?"
"Wilt thou at this time restore the kingdom to Israel?"
In order to answer these questions for others Jesus must
first have learned to answer them for himself. Naturally

the character of agriculture as process supplied him with some material for reply.

It is this element of growth in connection with the idea of the kingdom that has provided a convenient escape from the more unwelcome apocalyptic view. Do not the parables of Jesus deal with the kingdom? Do they not represent it as slow fruition rather than as cataclysm? And may not Jesus have thought of the kingdom as present as well as future? Instead of the affirmative answers expected by these questions one may point out rather that several of these parables are concerned exactly with that most apocalyptic of ancient metaphors—the harvest. The decisive outcome, the relation of the end to the beginning, are much more their concern than the intervening process. The extensive or intensive transformation found in the full-grown mustard tree or in the dough when thoroughly impregnated with yeast, the final and decisive difference of character and of fate between the wheat and the tares, the fruitfulness of the good soil contrasted with fruitlessness variously caused in the trodden soil, the shallow soil, and the weedy soil—such are among the lessons taught. Surely the shadow of a day of judgment is conspicuous here, as in the case of the fruitless fig tree or of the wicked husbandmen who withhold the fruit. Can it be that the feature of the parables which, even before the term "realized eschatology" was invented, was relied on to water down a too futuristic interpretation of the kingdom of God, confirms rather the apocalyptic emphasis upon the future?

Another recurrent feature of the parables, though one less often noted, is the motif of an absentee master. The point of several parables depends on the behavior of servants or subjects in an interval of separation or at a distance from their overlord. Let me quote some beginnings:

Mk. 12:1. A man planted a vineyard, and set an hedge about it, and digged a winevat, and built a tower, and let it out to husbandmen and went into a far country (ἀπεδήμησε).

Mk. 13:34. As a man taking a far journey (ἀπόδημος) who left his house, and gave authority to his servants, and to every man his work, and commanded the porter to watch.

Mt. 24:45 (= Lk. 12:42). Who then is a faithful and wise servant, whom his lord hath made ruler over his household, to give them their food in due season? Blessed is that servant whom his lord when he cometh (ἐλθών) shall find so doing.

Mt. 25:14, 15. As a man travelling into a far country (ἀποδημῶν) called his own servants, and delivered unto them his goods . . . to each according to his ability, and absented himself (ἀπεδήμησεν).

Lk. 19:12. A certain nobleman went into a far country (εἰς χώραν μακράν) to receive for himself a kingdom and to return, and he called his ten servants, etc.

In all these cases the master separates himself from those responsible to him by extensive intervals of time and place. Only in one case does the representative of God remain, while the representative of men goes away. That is the prodigal son who left his father and went himself into a far country (ἀπεδήμησεν εἰς χώραν μακράν, Lk. 15:13).

What do we make of this feature of the gospels? It is easy to see its congeniality to the early church. They were living in precisely such circumstances—awaiting their Lord's return. Their behavior before that *parousia* and particularly at that *parousia*—whose date was no more predictable than a thief's coming—was all important, since then their fate would be decided, like the servants', either with rewards or with punishments. No matter how familiar absentee landlordism was to the economic life of the Galilee of Jesus' time—and the contemporary papyri from neighboring Egypt now show us how extensive it was—its conspicuous place in the gospels is easily attributed to a subsequent apocalypticism. We have evidence that the early Christians were concerned with such matters. The parables of the Shepherd of Hermas continue the use of the same *motif* well down into the second century. Even variations in early Christian thought of the Lord's return may be reflected in the gospel parables. Certainly the unforeseen and trying delay of the *parousia* is well indicated by such phrases as "into a distant country" (Luke 19:12), and "after a long time" (Matt. 25:19); or by the servant's excuse "My lord delays" (his return, Matt. 24:48 = Luke 12:45). The seemingly extraneous elements in Luke's statements about the purpose of the nobleman's journey as getting a kingdom, and the deputation of his subjects after him to prevent his success, and his ruthless treatment of this disaffection, though thoroughly realistic by contemporary Herodian history—even these are appropriate to the theory of the secondary character of this feature.

But suppose this feature is original with Jesus and entirely authentic. In the case last mentioned the kingship may be a secondary feature, or, if one likes, a Jewish rather than a Christian trait, since the Jewish rabbis had their king parables; but the whole setting of an absentee master is integral to these stories and, if the parables go back to Jesus, that feature goes back too. In that case we have an unexpected disclosure of his viewpoint. Instead of the comforting presence of God he seems to teach the absence of God. Life, then, is not and cannot be the experience of uninterrupted fellowship and communion with the great Taskmaster. Rather one must live *as though* seeing him that is invisible, remembering his strict demands and our responsibility, and waiting through the present interim until the *parousia*. Much has been said about the ethics of Jesus as interim ethics, but much clearer from these parables comes the notion of an absentee God. Like the apocalyptic term *parousia*, they remind us that normally we are on our own and alone. For long intervals we have no contact with the one to whom we are responsible. He is in a distant country and there is no certainty that he will return soon. Our business is to live as we should live, but without him. Normal rectitude, fidelity, diligence, are expected of us and not emergency behavior. Blessed is the servant whom his master, when he cometh, shall find so doing. This absence goes far beyond the intermittent dullness of contact to which even the mystics confess. It is frankly non-mystical, and holds out no promise of a realized experience of God in this life.

This feature of Jesus' thought about God is of course not the whole story but it has been overshadowed by excessive emphasis on other features. In the parable of the Prodigal Son, as we have noted already, the father does not go away—the separation is due rather to the son, and of course the same is true of the lost sheep. Here is not divine absence, but our waywardness. Not only so, but in these parables we find a more generous and loving and forgiving person than in the stern master of the

servants. The latter element is not to be forgotten though
some exegetes make their effort to get away from it. Well
attested is the remark of the servant that the master is
austere and arbitrary. The Greek adjectives mean rigid
or harsh. His demands are unexpected and unauthorized.
The master himself admits that this is true. In other
parables a like strictness is depicted and perhaps from
the same point of view we should understand the rather
hard sayings about the prudence of the unjust steward.
Even his own master commends his shrewd self-interest,
which he exhibits upon learning that he is to be dis-
charged.

Is it not possible that these (to us) less welcome phases
of God were as real to Jesus as the more pleasant ones?
Do we indulge in wishful thinking when we say that the
loving Father is central in Jesus' teaching? To the by-
standers in the parables even generous acts are arbitrary
and unreasonable, and as a bystander in life Jesus may
well have felt that history in its treatment of men was
often harsh, arbitrary, unsympathetic and unintelligible.
He could not deny that it was like those agricultural
overlords who reap where they do not sow or those finan-
ciers who collect money that they never deposited. Suppose life is like that, what then? One must still carry on
bravely and faithfully. One need not expect to understand
now, nor to have any promise of a near and satisfactory
adjustment. In the end it may be well, but we are not at
the end and we may live long without knowing. We may
even die with the same last words upon our lips, "My
God, my God, why hast thou forsaken me?"

In spite of what I said earlier disowning certain eschatological emphases of the evangelists, what I have de-

scribed about the parables of harvest and of the re-
turning master suggests that Jesus himself thinks in
apocalyptic terms. At this point I know the modern world
inclines to part company with him. Even here I think
Jesus is more nearly right. Rather than twist the gospels
to our modern evolutionary concepts of science, I
would inquire whether religious experience as distinct
from science does not confirm the standpoint of the parables; for experience deals with things as they seem rather than with what they can be discovered historically
to have been. The harvest looks unexpected and sudden,
because the farmer quite properly is not watching for it
but is attending to other things. The master's absence
and sudden unpredictable return is merely the way it
looks to the servant. Actually those on the inside may
know otherwise. The farmer knows that without his
attention the seed is growing of itself from stage to stage.
The master is not, in his own view, either absent or sudden. The theologian, especially the mystic, prefers to
talk of the "seeming" absence of God, and to distinguish
in God's dealings with men between their humanly inscrutable and unpredictable character and their orderly
and natural place in the plans of God.

Even history and science increasingly allow us now-
adays to sympathize with the apocalyptic viewpoint of the
gospels. Many New Testament scholars who had re-
sisted Schweitzer's views because they seemed to make
Jesus unrealistic in his cataclysmic view of history admitted that since the outbreak of the First World War
they found apocalypticism more congenial and have
moved over towards the eschatalogical school. We are
none of us so sure as were our fathers that

Through the ages an increasing purpose runs,
And the thoughts of men are widen'd with the process of the
suns.

At the same time scientists and philosophers are making
more and more room in their systems for discontinuity
instead of mechanical continuity, for mutation instead
of routine. Nature itself moves towards revolution and
convulsion.

The main consideration, however, is that we should
recollect that Jesus is not giving a philosophy of history
or a philosophy of science, but homely advice on human
experience. We may possibly, perhaps naturally, read
religious experience in ways different from the findings
of science, and the man in the street today has the problem not of the secret processes of the ages but of personal
response to the situations that arise. These situations
often are in effect for him sudden and unforeseeable.
They come "in an hour that ye think not," "like a thief
in the night," and the advice of Jesus is still humanly
sound, "Watch, for ye know not."[3]

Whatever one may think of the parables of Jesus as
indicative of his thought of God, they may be accepted as
showing what he observed among men. Their lifelike-
ness still charms us, even in spite of their occasional
exotic or antique traits. I shall limit myself to one feature of their human verisimilitude—and again a less attractive one, men's tendency to find excuses. Corresponding to the divine strictness that has been mentioned is

[3] See "The Eschatology of the Synoptic Gospels: its Fidelity to Religious Experience," by W. L. Sperry, in the *Harvard Theological Re-
view,* V (1912), 385–395.

the futility of human efforts to evade or to find excuse. The parables show, however, this characteristic human trait in action. Men are like that.

No doubt the parable tradition before Jesus' time may have contained such elements. One of the earliest of Hebrew parables contains one of the commonest of excuses—that of being otherwise occupied. It is the invented story told by an anonymous prophet to the king of Israel, when the latter had allowed the defeated Syrian king Ben-hadad to get off with a soft peace. Speaking as if it were his own experience, the prophet narrates:

> Thy servant went into the midst of the battle; and behold a man turned aside, and brought a man unto me, and said, Keep this man: if by any means he be missing, then shall thy life be for his life, or else thou shalt pay a talent of silver. And as thy servant was busy here and there, he was gone.[4]

While he was busy here and there his prisoner escaped. Such excuses are not, so far as I know, characteristic of the rabbinic parables. No doubt they were characteristic of Jesus' experience. Quite outside the parables our gospels tell of the men who wished to follow Jesus, but were deterred. Whether the reasons given were reasons or excuses one cannot always tell. There was the rich man who was told to sell first all that he had—no doubt a pretty good reason for not following Jesus. There were those who evaded their duty to care for their parents by the subterfuge of the religious vow—saying to their father or mother: "That which you might have had from me for your support is Corban"—that is, dedicated to God. But there were those who conversely used their

---

[4] 1 Kings 20:39, 40.

family as a prior claim—"Lord, suffer me first to go and bury my father," or, "I will follow thee, Lord; but first suffer me to bid farewell to them that are at my house." No doubt Jesus was fully aware from experience of the interfering reasons in men's failure of the highest. Whether cumbered like Martha about much serving, or choked with riches, or held by family ties or for other reasons, they made what Dante called "the great refusal."

The parable of the sower, at least as the gospels themselves interpret it, is a beautiful description of the conditioning causes of spiritual unproductivity—temptation, tribulation, anxiety, pleasure, wealth, desire. Luke elsewhere speaks of hearts weighed down with surfeiting and drunkenness and secular anxieties. In the parable of the good Samaritan, on the other hand, we are allowed to guess for ourselves the reasons why both the priest and the Levite passed by the wounded victim on the other side, detouring the duty of compassion.

The most familiar story of excuses is in Luke's parable of the great supper. According to oriental custom the invitation sent out well in advance was repeated on the day of the meal:

He sent forth his slave at suppertime to say to those that were invited: Come, for things are now ready. And they all with one consent began to make excuses. The first said unto him, I have bought a field, and I must needs go and see it: I pray thee have me excused. And another said, I have bought five yoke of oxen, and I go to prove them; I pray thee have me excused. And another said, I have married a wife and therefore I cannot come.

Possibly some of this circumstantial picture is due to Luke rather than to Jesus. Matthew's gospel puts it much more simply. There the guests "slighted" (ἀμελήσαντες) the second invitation and went their ways, one to his own farm, another to his merchandise, while the rest laid hold of the messengers and treated them shamefully and killed them. This last clause carries us into a quite different analogy, from neglect into active hostility, like the wicked husbandmen who contrived not to pay the share croppers' dues. If the deprecatory phrase "have me excused" is, as has been claimed, a Latinism, that is probably more likely due to outside tradition than to Palestinian origin. As I have noted elsewhere it is Luke alone, who suggests—and that three times—that a wife may be an excuse or rather a positive hindrance. The benedict does not say politely—I pray thee have me excused, but bluntly, "Therefore I cannot come."

The other excuses in parables need only be listed. The ill-behaved slave who acts riotously and maltreats his fellows says in his heart simply, "My master tarries." The foolish virgins are no doubt inconvenienced by the bridegroom's delay, but their plight is due to their own unpreparedness. The wise virgins had oil in their vessels with their lamps. Of course unreadiness is elsewhere emphasized in the teachings of Jesus, the unlit lamp and the ungirt loin, but it is no valid excuse. It could have been avoided. The householder, roused at midnight to lend some bread, though his hesitation is finally overcome, does plead that the door is now shut and his children are with him in the bed. As with many other excuses there is no denying the facts asserted. They may be true enough but are they relevant? I have already mentioned that the man who failed to invest his master's money is not contradicted when he gives as his reason that his master was notoriously strict and arbitrary. All the more reason for doing his duty—I will judge you out of your own mouth (Luke), you knew that I was . . . , therefore you ought to have . . . (Matthew) or, so why didn't you . . . ? (Luke)

Perhaps according to ancient standards the unjust steward's words, "I cannot dig, to beg I am ashamed," were more of a natural excuse than a valid reason. Somewhat more complicated in its context, but quite striking, is the reason given by those who, on the day of judgment, are accused by the king of not having ministered to him. They did not realize any more than those who had done so that services rendered to one of the least of the little ones were done to him, and so in tones of injured innocence they ask, "Sir, when did we see you hungry or thirsty or a stranger or naked, or sick, or in prison and not minister to you?"

Once more the prodigal son offers an exception, and one of the most attractive features of the story is precisely his frank sincerity in admitting his guilt. He seeks no excuse or alibi. He will neither palliate nor extenuate his fault. Efforts to excuse, deny, or conceal would have done no good with his jealous brother, with his father they would have proved either useless or unnecessary. As the publican in the temple prays simply "God, be merciful to me a sinner" the younger son throws himself on his father's mercy. He is not ashamed to work either abroad or at home, he does not presume on a social prestige he no longer deserves and he does not beg off or excuse himself. He manfully admits to God and man that he is in the wrong: *"Peccavi,* I have sinned before heaven and in thy sight."

As one reviews the array of excuses in Jesus' parables it becomes an appalling commentary on human nature, as well as a striking disclosure of his insight into human nature. We still have with us persons who are too busy, or too lazy, too slow, or too much in a hurry, too improvident, too unaware, or too proud—to do as they should do. They can use the perverseness of the world as an excuse, or the unexpected delay of the time of reckoning, and if on the other hand the day of reckoning finds them unprepared, they will not recognize that it is their fault for having put other interests first that should have been secondary. In the light of the cumulative evidence most of this sensitiveness to human frailty goes back to the utterances of Jesus himself.

Let us return to the evangelists' theory that the parables were intended to conceal, and ask what is the reason for Jesus' use of these figures in case the evangelists' theory is erroneous? As Matthew says, Why speakest thou in parables? Two answers now suggest themselves. One is that other contemporary teachers used them and that Jesus' hearers were accustomed to illustrations of this kind and were experienced in interpreting them. Jesus unconsciously, like all of us, follows the practices of his environment. The other reason is the probability that Jesus himself was accustomed to think this way. The illustrations were the original sources of his own insights rather than adduced or employed to confirm insights independently arrived at. Perhaps what he says in this connection to his disciples is applicable to himself. Through the parables "it is given to know the mysteries of the kingdom of God." The facts of religion and of ethics may be directly observed in nature and in men since all of life is homogeneous and mutually analogous. Evidently at this point I am anticipating broader questions, some of which will be discussed in the fifth chapter.

CHAPTER IV

WHAT IS THIS? NEW TEACHING!

The originality or uniqueness of Jesus is frequently asserted. The texts commonly appealed to are John 8:46, "never man so spake," and Mark 1:27, "What is this? a new teaching!" But when the matter is further analyzed three questions arise. Is the originality or uniqueness possible to prove or is it an *a priori* hypothesis? Is it desirable? And wherein does originality or novelty lie?

The uniqueness of Jesus may be claimed on some metaphysical grounds. Those who assume he was more than human expect that fact to result in original or unfamiliar ideas on his part. They say, "God's thoughts are not our thoughts." By hypothesis, then, what Jesus said must have been new. In fact they seem to assume that the new is true and that there are no such things as old truths or new falsehoods. They equate divinity with novelty. Even so it would be better if they would attempt to establish first the historical uniqueness of Jesus and then draw the metaphysical inference. Otherwise they may be found arguing in a circle.

Any assertion of absolute uniqueness or originality can hardly rest on full knowledge, especially for a figure so ancient as Jesus. Whenever one says, "Jeremiah was the first person in history to think this or that" or "Plato was the only person to do so and so," we really mean the first

or only one that we know of. If we go beyond that we are
guilty of the fallacy of the argument from silence. We
employ our own ignorance in the interests of some superlative claim—of priority or originality or uniqueness. It is natural to do so but it is not arguing from ade-
quate historical evidence.

One often discovers that what seems original in another is merely what is unfamiliar to ourselves. It proves
our own limitations rather than the other's unusual, not
to say unique, character. As I listen today to one whose
field of specialization is not my own, I find it impossible
to judge how far he speaks with the consensus of others,
how far he is original and independent of the ruling
opinions in this field. So also unless I know the whole of
the ancient world—and that is now impossible—I can
speak of the originality of any ancient individual only as
an impression subject to the limitations of my own ignorance. At this distance what seems to us distinctive in
Jesus may have been to his hearers commonplace and
vice versa. Modern scholars both Jewish and Christian
have learned how much there is in common between the
early classics of their religions. They are in a better position to relate Jesus within the circle of his age than
were those older scholars who were always concerned to
find the maximum contrasts between Jesus and his opponents. Possibly for Christians the sheer familiarity of
some things in the gospels sometimes obscures their original novelty. Sometimes it does quite the reverse, for it
gives a false impression of their distinctively Christian
flavor.

One argument for the thesis that Jesus was original
can be found in the power of his influence. If the Chris-

tian movement is to be accounted for, a unique personality seems demanded, a biological sport in the process of
history, not merely a revival of old prophetism, or the
fortunate concatenation of forces in the Levantine culture of the First Century. The idea that new grows out
of old is not so popular as the idea that nothing new can
exist without a really new factor, and in the case of Christianity a novelty commensurate to the strength and lon-
gevity of the movement is sought in the person of
Jesus.

A further argument would be the hostility he aroused.
I have often wondered just how different a man must be
to be hanged for it. We are increasingly aware in modern
times of the Jewishness of Jesus. He moved within the
field of thought current in First Century Judaism. If he
had been a total alien he might have been less suspected
and feared. The bitterest controversy is often over the
narrowest margin. There must be some difference between enemies, rivalry of conflicting self-interest if nothing more; but it need not be great or significant. The
differentia of Jesus that would estrange the Jews might
be quite different from what would "found" the church,
and in neither case need his position have been very different from the position of other Jews, either quantitatively or qualitatively.

That Jesus incurred the hostility of the Jewish leaders
and that they were ultimately responsible for his death,
though on a Roman cross, may be accepted as historical
facts. They do not carry evidence of commensurate originality. Independence, or—if you will—unorthodoxy,
might be a more suitable term, though of course the conventional and orthodox often charge their opponents

with novelty. So Socrates was charged with bringing in "new gods," a *motif* that is reflected in the Athens scene in the Christian Book of Acts, and in American Church History the dissentients have often been dubbed "New Lights." It is perhaps significant that in the gospels novelty is neither a claim of Jesus nor a charge of his opponents. There is plenty of room for difference of opinion within a circle of older ideas. Judaism was a varied religion with diverse factors of tradition and with divergent traits and opportunities for differing emphasis extending back into history.

Certainly claims of continuity and antiquity are much more likely to have been made for Jesus by his friends than the reverse. Since our gospels come from friendly sources they are unlikely to stress novelty and originality. Congenial to their own sincere view is the remark of the fawning insincere opponents: "Thou regardest not the person of men, but of a truth teachest the way of God." Independent, yes! but not necessarily radical or revolutionary. One tendency of early Christian tradition would be against exaggerating novelty in Jesus. This fact alone would make that feature in him difficult now to recognize or recover. Even when novelty in Christianity was regarded as an asset it had to compete with or combine with the still valid and valuable claim of antiquity. The early Christians were not indifferent to the advantage of a religion that could claim continuity with the past. They linked themselves to the Old Testament and like apologists of a later day were prepared to prove "Christianity as old as the Creation." Even in the gospels Jesus is sometimes represented as criticizing his opponents as innovators. "In the beginning it was not so," he says when they appeal to the Mosaic law of divorce. For the really recent doctrine of resurrection he himself appeals to ancient history. In argument, at least, Jesus and his opponents are alike in eschewing any confession of novelty.

Probably we come the nearest to an objective criterion of the originality of Jesus if we compare the gospel teaching with that of rabbinic literature. Even here subjective judgment, not to say prejudice, is eliminated with difficulty. We have, however, real historical data to go on. Of course the gospels may represent in part later Christianity rather than Jesus himself, just as the Mishna, Talmud and Midrash are later in actual recording and perhaps in viewpoint than the Judaism of the First Century. Where the two agree the gospels are prior, but not enough earlier to indicate that the Jewish material is borrowed from the Christian. Coincidence or earlier common inheritance—albeit unrecorded—is a more plausible explanation of similarity. Uniqueness or originality are therefore largely ruled out. The differences are the things distinctive or characteristic of either side. This, indeed, is the spirit in which many Christian and Jewish scholars now approach the subject. As was to be expected their findings even among Jews or among Christians do not always agree and hence sometimes cancel each other out. On both sides the differences between the teaching of Jesus and of Judaism have been exaggerated. The Jewishness of Jesus is a common phrase. One recalls Wellhausen's remark: "Jesus was not a Christian: he was a Jew. He did not preach a new faith, but taught men to do the will of God; and in his opinion, as also in that of the

Jews, the will of God was to be found in the Law of Moses and in the other books of Scripture."[1]

Perhaps no one has attempted more honestly or with better knowledge of Judaism to indicate the differentia of the gospels than has Claude G. Montefiore, in a series of thoughtful studies,[2] and his discriminating suggestions will be pondered with interest by all students of this problem. Yet he insists quite rightly that the matter is complicated. He can select a few gospel sayings and attitudes which are hardly paralleled by the Rabbis, that seem unfamiliar to one who comes from reading Talmud and Midrash; but he is aware that the comparison needed is between what is characteristic of each party. For example the mere absence from Jesus' teaching of a large amount of the material in the Talmud may be more important than any plus that we can discover in the gospels. I think it was the same Wellhausen who is credited with replying to the Jews who asserted that every teaching of Jesus could be found in the Talmud, "Yes, but how much more!"

Certainly one distinctive feature of Jesus' teaching is the sense of urgency which the apocalyptic outlook gives his words, and according to Montefiore there is a notable intensity and glow about them. He writes:[3]

---

[1] *Einleitung in die drei ersten Evangelien*, 1905, p. 113. The same expression occurs with slight alteration in the second edition, 1911, p. 102.

[2] Beside his article in the *Hibbert Journal*, xxviii, October, 1929, pp. 98–111, on "The Originality of Jesus," reprinted in part in T. S. Kepler, *Contemporary Thinking about Jesus*, 1944, pp. 379–386, see *The Synoptic Gospels*, 2nd edit., 1927, pp. cxxxix–cxlii; *Some Elements of the Religious Teaching of Jesus*, 1910; *The Old Testament and After*, 1923; *Rabbinic Literature and Gospel Teachings*, 1930.

[3] C. G. Montefiore, "The Originality of Jesus," *Hibbert Journal*, xxviii, October, 1929, p. 109.

. . . I would like to illustrate my meaning by a short reference to the Beatitudes, especially as we find them in Matthew, without considering whether they are more or less authentic in Matthew than in Luke. The Beatitudes as a whole seem more than each one taken separately. There is a certain glow and intensity about them which seems new and distinctive. We can find Rabbinic parallels to each of them, but as a whole they seem original. If I be asked, "In what does the impression left by the Beatitudes in Matthew seem to you peculiar and original?", I find it very hard to put that impression into words. Perhaps it is a feeling as if all religion were concentrated and expressed in a certain condition of soul, which manifests itself in gentleness and pity and love and the patient endurance of wrong; in a certain peacefulness, which is also capable of utmost heroism and sacrifice, in a certain glow and enthusiasm, which produce a peculiar and indomitable happiness. Before the ideal of this religion all else appears to fade away; all that is external and institutional; all that is civic and political; all that has to do with beauty and knowledge; all that makes for the careful and orderly and gradual removal of evils by intelligent forethought or wise legislation; all conceptions of progress. All these things are good and are necessary, and yet the Beatitudes seem to teach the one thing needful which is more needful than any of them, and which goes both before them and after them. The Beatitudes seem to illustrate the unqualified absoluteness of the teaching of Jesus. . . .

Insofar as Jesus was more independent of the law than his contemporaries he seems to have been original. But since he did not break with the law entirely he was less consistent than his opponents. This is quite clear to Jewish scholars whether like Montefiore they praise Jesus for his bold words, "Nothing that goes into a man from out-

side can defile him," or whether like Klausner they condemn him for his irresponsible indifference to the maintenance in the world of a distinctive Jewish culture.
Probably to some of us consistency will seem no more
important in itself than originality, and probably in
other fields also the latter can be had only at the cost of
the former. Speaking of Jesus' bold working (i. e., curing)
on the sabbath, Montefiore says:[4]

. . . It has been suggested that it was something of both a
moral and an intellectual fault on the part of the Rabbis that
they did not appreciate and sympathise with Jesus' point of
view about the Sabbath directly it was clearly explained to
them. I can hardly agree with this suggestion. The Rabbis
were, in truth, more consistent than Jesus, and if you take
the Law at its face value, as the perfect will of God, there is
a great deal to be said for the Rabbinic view as to how con-
flicts between Sabbath law and moral law are to be decided.
The conception of the Law and of Scripture, to which the
attitude of Jesus points forward, was not theoretically
reached till modern times. One could hardly expect the Rabbis to be 1900 years before their time, and if the suggestion
were right, the high originality of Jesus and of his glorious
inconsistency would, perhaps, even be diminished.

More important for us here is it to note the areas in
which Montefiore does not find the originality often
claimed for Jesus:

I need hardly waste time in dealing with, and disposing of
certain old oppositions such as that to the Rabbis God is a
King, to Jesus He is a Father, that the Rabbis fear God, Jesus
loves Him, that to the Rabbis God is far, to Jesus He is near,

[4] *Loc. cit.,* p. 103.

that the Rabbinic religion is one of vengeance and severity, the Gospel religion one of love and pity, and so on. Serious students have happily advanced beyond such crude and sweeping contrasts. . . .

There are many doctrines in the Gospels which an ordinary Christian commentary would speak of as highly original, but which I either cannot admit to be so, or which I could only admit to be so with tedious qualifications. Such would be the combination of love for God and love of man in Mark xii. 30, 31, the denial of the doctrine that suffering betokens sin, the positive form of the Golden Rule, a deliberate universalism, and faith.[5]

Granted that something about Jesus seemed unfamiliar or novel, what was it? The passage in Mark already cited has a context not to be ignored. It can be translated: "What is this? A new teaching with authority. He commands even the unclean spirits and they obey him." Earlier in the same paragraph Mark wrote: "They were astonished at his teaching, for he taught them as having authority and not as the scribes." Matthew applies this to a whole collection of sayings of Jesus about the Jewish religion, the Sermon on the Mount. Mark, however, and with him Luke, indicate rather a contrast not so much in content of teaching as in manner, and perhaps concretely in the accompanying powerful credentials of successful exorcism. Not originality of doctrine, nor even apocalyptic tensity, but sheer miraculous sanction may have seemed the novelty.

Many modern thinkers would prefer to suppose that the differentia of Jesus was in his person, his authority and his manner rather than in the substance of his teach-

[5] *Loc. cit.*, pp. 104, 108.

ing. Even in the ancient times he was reported to have expressed a conservative attitude to the law—he came not to break it but to keep it. The strand of loyalty to Judaism is a conspicuous one in Matthew, and yet even Luke, who is less concerned with Judaism either pro or con than the other evangelists, apparently accepts Jesus as no revolutionary, but as one who can quote *con amore,* "The old is good."

Certainly one cannot dissociate a man from his teaching, and if Jesus' distinctive teaching were reinforced by his own practice the total impression would be enhanced. Christians assume that this was the case, but apart from his teachings unambiguous evidence on the character of Jesus is somewhat scanty. The teachings themselves have a certain unity of suggestion, but they are not point by point confirmed by examples of Jesus' own conformity to them. Since actions speak more loudly than words, appeal to Jesus' acts for evidence is natural. The gospel narratives do not often disclose the motives of Jesus, nor were they written by persons sensitive to the criterion of moral originality. Thus, speaking of Jesus' great teaching on love of enemies, Montefiore remarks: [6]

Jesus is to be regarded as the first great Jewish teacher to frame such a sentence. . . . Yet how much more telling his injunction would have been if we had *a single story* about his doing good to and praying for a single Rabbi or Pharisee! Luke xxiii. 34 is of doubtful range and of doubtful authenticity.

I have said that Jesus probably did not covet originality and if his teachings were novel he may not have been specially conscious of that fact. Indeed, the ancient world whether Jewish or pagan shows little evidence of an interest in originality in the sense in which modern persons apply the term in praise. The Greeks are an example of people who, relying heavily on tradition and commonplace, paradoxically developed quite original achievements.[7] Probably the same could be said of the innovators among the Hebrew prophets. Indeed, even in modern art and literature there is a strong adherence to forms and conventions and the repetition of commonplace ideas compatible with originality of combination and development.[8] We must distinguish in fact between originality in science, where discovery and invention may be claimed as something wholly novel, and originality in literature or art, where a somewhat superficial criterion has in modern times been established by which the term original is applied to novelty of presentation and combination though the themes are old. In the case of religion and morals originality is bound to be more of this latter kind. The subject matter does not permit of complete innovation. The contrast is well expressed by Professor E. F. Scott.[9]

There is a grave confusion in most people's minds as to what constitutes originality in the sphere of morals and religion. More especially in our own time we have been dazzled by the triumphs of scientific discovery, and assume, more or less consciously, that all original thinking must conform to this type. Newton, Darwin, Pasteur were obviously original.

[7] F. R. Earp, *The Way of the Greeks*, 1929, Chapter I.

[8] J. L. Lowes, *Convention and Revolt in Poetry*, 1919, Chapter III.

[9] E. F. Scott, "The Originality of Jesus' Ethical Teaching," *Journal of Biblical Literature*, 48, 1929, pp. 111–112.

They definitely enlarged our field of knowledge; they brought to light principles of nature which no one had guessed before. So we take for granted that if Jesus was original he also must have contributed certain ideas which were specifically new. For an ethical teacher, however, this was impossible. From the beginning men had been concerned with the great moral questions. The true answers had been forced on them by all the experiences of life and by the very conditions of man's being. Their judgments had indeed been warped by custom and tradition and strange beliefs, but there has been no religion outside of mere savagery in which the principles of right living were not in some degree recognised. In Judaism they had been discerned with marvellous insight by a long succession of great thinkers, and a noble and comprehensive moral code had been built up, on the basis of the ten commandments. Jesus therefore had all his materials ready to his hand. It is the very proof of his originality that he was content to work with them as they were. The temptation of inferior moralists, as of second-rate poets and artists, is to despise what lies before them and strain after novelty and paradox. These cheap substitutes for originality are painfully familiar to us in our own day. Jesus did not resort to them. He perceived that everything was given in those truths which men knew already. Over all his teaching might be written the great text, "Say not, who will ascend into heaven? who will go down into the deeps? for the word is very near thee, in thy heart and in thy mouth." So he took over the traditional ethic, and yet in doing so transformed it into something new.

Indeed, we may well inquire whether in the field of religion and morals novelty has any inherent value. Is it not quite as important to select and emphasize the best in the old as to elaborate the new? What Jesus taught was probably independent and distinctive. It was no doubt effectively put, fresh and striking in expression, and for some hearers it had the confirmation of an echoing inner response. But complete novelty would have been a doubtful asset. Admitting that Jesus had distinctive ideas G. Bernard Shaw once wrote:[10]

I do not imply that these doctrines were peculiar to Christ. A doctrine peculiar to one man would be only a craze unless its comprehension depended on a development of human faculty so rare that only one exceptionally gifted man possessed it. But even in that case it would be useless, because impossible of spreading.

We shall do well not to seek with great desire for the originality of Jesus or to exaggerate what we find. It will provide no criterion of his greatness or of his contribution to history. The most original persons in modern society are rightly or wrongly to be found in our institutions for the insane. In Jesus we shall look for what was distinguished if not distinctive, what was characteristic and *sui generis,* rather than for something that would seem to us or his contemporaries original or novel. Fidelity to the best of the past, moral maturity, good balance and sensible judgment are rare enough at all times and may well have elicited in the First Century, as in our own, surprise and deserved praise.

Perhaps more nearly accurate than the words novel, original, unique, for describing any differentia of Jesus, would be such adjectives as radical, intense, extreme. His contemporaries may have found such terms as ap-

[10] *Androcles and the Lion,* Preface. Published by Constable, London, 1916, and by Brentano, New York, 1916. Copyright by G. Bernard Shaw, 1916. Used by permission.

plicable to him as we find them today. Many thoughtful and well informed writers about him have applied such epithets. To the modern Jewish writers acquainted with the religion of his contemporaries he seems extreme, intense or one-sided, as citations from them in this volume show. So Bousset says: "Jesus was fond of exhibiting things in all their forbidding harshness, one-sidedness and crudity. . . . A better understanding of some of the sharpest and most daring sayings of Jesus is obtained when we grasp the fact that they are consciously one-sided and paradoxical. . . . What he preached was the ethics of heroism, of absolute unquestioning enthusiasm . . . . His magnificent and unbounded moral one-sidedness did constitute a danger to the maintenance of law and order. . . . What Jesus had to do was to break a passage for the higher moral view, to liberate the higher world from the lower one of every day. And then even one-sidedness may be in season."[11] To other Christians some other terms would seem applicable. They would say that he took religion seriously—but so I think did his enemies; or that he followed the divine command logically to its ultimate implications—but so surely did the scribes and Pharisees. Without trying to give this aspect of his character and teaching a name let us look at some of the evidence.

In spite of his critical attitude towards Judaism Matthew assigns to Jesus words like these: "Not one jot or tittle of the law shall fail." "Except your righteousness exceeds that of the scribes and Pharisees you shall not enter the kingdom of Heaven." Two of the six compari-

[11] W. Bousset, *Jesus*, English Translation, G. P. Putnam's Sons, 1906, pp. 32, 45, 142, 144.

sons between Jesus' teaching and that of men of old carry prohibitions of the decalogue from acts of murder or adultery to feelings of anger or lust. It is customary to say that Jesus taught the inwardness of religion, the infinite value of the individual soul, the necessity of absolute devotion to his cause, the unconditional demands for self-sacrifice, the unbounded scope of divine love. According to Montefiore one of the unique things both in Jesus' teaching about God and in his own example was that love involved seeking out the lost. He also describes Jesus' teaching about divine fatherhood as "an old familiar doctrine" of the rabbis in "a high degree of purity, warmth and concentration." [12]

In all this, Jesus' relation to other standards and practices is defined not by negatives and opposites but by the use of the comparative or, more commonly, the superlative degree. If others forgive seven times Jesus counsels forgiveness "seventy times seven" times. If others do good to friends Jesus would have us do good to enemies. In this context occurs the much discussed injunction, "Be ye perfect," and perhaps it is best understood as an expression of precisely this radical temper of Jesus.[13]

Are there any explanations of such a phenomenon about Jesus? Why does he seem such an extremist? Something could be set down to a habit of language. He was given to overstatements,—in his case not a personal idiosyncrasy, but a characteristic of the oriental world.[14] It

[12] *Some Elements of the Religious Teaching of Jesus*, 1910, p. 93.
[13] I am glad to find myself concurring in these paragraphs with an essay of the late James Hardy Ropes on "The Religious Radicalism of Jesus" posthumously published in *Crozer Quarterly*, xxiv, 1947, pp. 113–119.
[14] See C. C. Douglas, *Overstatement in the Gospels*, 1931.

is largely literary, hyperbole as a figure of speech, and since his sayings have other clearly poetic traits like metaphor and simile, these must be regarded as a kind of poetic license. In some cases we may be misled by the difference between Aramaic and English idiom as when "not" is used in the sense "not merely," or "and not" is equivalent to "more than."

Again, Jesus may have had reasons in the special conditions for such emphasis. If his sayings were originally occasional and to individuals, any tendency on the part of early reporters or modern readers to generalize them makes them automatically much more sweeping and unrestricted. Few of them would seem even to the most sober and sophisticated moralist not to have on occasion real validity, or to need any apology or qualification if thought of as *ad hoc* advice. We can trace in our gospels and manuscripts a tendency to generalization on the part of later Christians, and, I may add, a consequent and corresponding tendency to tone down the arduousness of the advice, thus compensating for the difficulties of regarding it as applicable *semper, ubique, ab omnibus*.

Undoubtedly the ancient or modern Christian has found the example and teaching of Jesus more congenial in proportion as they are fitted into a perspective of crisis. If Jesus himself regarded the time as short, the kingdom of God near, he had every good reason to make his message urgent. Urgency affects the content of the message too. All obstacles, all alternatives, must be ruthlessly put aside. Among them are not merely inward faults and sins, but kindred and possessions, an offending hand or foot and even life itself. Probably we can never find out what Jesus would have said or what many of those that stood by would have reported him as saying, if it had been plain in the First Century that not for at least 1900 years would the kingdom of God come with power, in the literal manner now predicted in the gospels.

Finally, much that Jesus said was doubtless not merely occasional, but controversial. It was his answer to situations that were extreme and needed extreme corrective. We may be sure that it was in response to immoderate hate that he recommended love, and that his words on forgiveness were not intended for persons already of a reconciling spirit. The gospels reflect a milieu of strong tension. There was entrenched a party, a code, a standard, against which Jesus strongly reacted. Every reaction—to invert the common saying—has an equal and opposite action. Jesus' reactions, if strong, are an indication of the strength he felt in the positions that he criticized. He was equally vigorous on his side, perhaps more so, as befits "his Majesty's loyal opposition."

Whatever the reasons for the extremism of Jesus the fact is there and ought not to be minimized or ignored. Historical or temperamental explanations do not explain this feature away. Jesus' uncompromising demands are part of the historical record, and probably belong to the actual personality. Whether we like them or not they seem characteristic of him. The morality he advocated was often merely the current morality, but intensified and unconditional, stated without qualification or reserve. Such radicalism, of course, was unwelcome to the responsible Jewish leaders. It ran counter to their necessary compromises and to their human concessions. It explains their hostility.

It explains also the attraction of Jesus. Other Jews,

especially the simple minded, the outcast, the disin-
herited, were attracted to it, though not all could follow
it to its end. There was an appeal in its sheer ruggedness,
in its demand for self-sacrifice even apart from the accompanying promise of reward. It conveyed an impression of assurance in the teacher, of assurance not secondhand and dependent on another source, but spontaneous and independent. I think that is what the Greek
ἐξουσία translated "authority" in the Gospels really means.
It is often associated with δύναμις, power. The idea of
something delegated or derived is too conspicuous in our
translation. Underived power rather than novelty in content was probably the impression which Jesus gave in his
teaching. His self-assurance and heroic radicalism were
well matched by his powerful influence over those dis-
tressed in mind, body or estate.

Chapter V

HOW KNOWETH THIS MAN?

Nothing annoys and offends certain Christians more than if one states the conviction that in a particular matter Jesus was probably right, or more generally that he was of such ethical maturity that his judgment was frequently right. They begin with the assumption that he was always right, and it seems to them to be the worst kind of arrogance and impiety to attempt to confirm his judgments. Compared with such patronizing approval, outright rejection of his standards would be no worse. In spite of this risk I wish in this chapter to call attention to certain recurrent features of the gospels which, if I correctly read them, would seem to me to indicate important and sound approaches to life's problems.

A good deal in a teacher's answer depends on the circumstances under which the answer is given. Jesus' teaching was probably much of it occasional, no matter how sententious it seems for a casual reply. Even the longer discourses in our gospels were probably not originally so delivered. Tradition has gathered up words spoken on many occasions. While some of Jesus' sayings are preserved with their original setting or pretty definitely imply that setting by their contents, for others the setting has been supplied by the imagination of the evangelist, or no setting at all is available. Thus we often are given the answers without the questions. For that reason any complete verdict on Jesus' teaching is bound to be precarious.

There are, however, a number of stories in the gospels which seem to indicate that on occasion Jesus deliberately refused to answer questions. However one interprets the peculiar reply attributed to him when on trial, "Thou sayest it," there is the statement in each one of the four gospels that to the persistent questioning of one of his judges he made no reply. The model for this may of course be not history but the prophecy of Isaiah 53:7:

As a lamb that is led to the slaughter,
And as a sheep that before the shearers is dumb,
So he opened not his mouth.

This "silence strike" is a game that two can play. Jesus recognizes the deadlock when he says, "If I tell you, ye will not believe, and if I ask you, ye will not answer."

There are, besides, the many passages which according to the evangelists' interpretation were questions staged to test Jesus with no friendly purpose. Jesus deliberately in these instances gives an evasive reply. One of them is:

"Is it lawful to give tribute to Caesar, or not?"

Another is concerning the woman taken in adultery:

In the law Moses commanded us to stone such: what then sayest thou? (John 8:5)

Another is the request for a sign (Mark 8:11 and parallels). Though in other cases the questions are directly answered even though said to be asked merely to tempt him (Mark 10:2; Luke 10:25; Matt. 22:35), the three mentioned are not vouchsafed a direct answer. Even John the Baptist's question, no doubt a friendly one, "Art thou he that should come or look we for another?" (Matt. 11:13–Luke 7:19) receives no direct reply. Again Jesus throws back upon the questioners a similar question of his own when asked by what authority he acted (Mark 11:28) or what a man must do to inherit eternal life (Luke 10:25). In Matthew 15 we have a similar return of question for question, though here the questions are complaints and the reply becomes a kind of *Tu quoque*:

Then there came to Jesus from Jerusalem Pharisees and scribes, saying, "Why do thy disciples transgress the tradition of the elders? for they wash not their hands when they eat bread." And he answered and said unto them, "Why do ye also transgress the commandment of God because of your tradition?"

When entreated to intervene in family quarrels between two brothers (Luke 12:13-15) or two sisters (Luke 10:38-42) Jesus refuses, and appears in each case to rebuke rather the complaining party.

Now all these passages may be interpreted in terms of the principle (mentioned hereafter) of Jesus' one-sided attention to the person he is speaking with. They indicate even in that case that he knew what he wanted. He was not prepared to let others state the issue or catch him on the horns of a dilemma of their own making. He had his own angle, his own paramount interest. Sometimes it could be expressed by direct reply to questions asked, sometimes it could be expressed by no reply, and sometimes the substitute question which he set, or the apparently irrelevant reply, was best calculated to divert attention of the questioner to a more significant issue.

We are all familiar with teachers who are annoyingly non-committal or evasive. Whatever their pedagogical purpose, it is not necessarily the same as that of Jesus. I think there was nothing merely formal or intentional in the cases I have mentioned; they represent his settled interests and emphases over against the issues that were presented to him.

One of the reassuring features of the synoptic gospels is the fact that the questions asked Jesus can so often be identified as the exact issues of his time and place. The Pharisees and Sadducees differed on the resurrection of the dead. The latter's question was an attempt to confront Jesus with a *reductio ad absurdum*. The schools and rabbis were often asking, Which is the great commandment? Is it lawful to cure the sick on the sabbath? May a man divorce his wife for any cause? Tribute to Caesar or the marriage of divorced persons were by no means academic questions only, as the anti-Roman zealots or the disciples of John the Baptist could have told us with emphasis. In some cases Jesus' answers, like the questions, are known from other sources to have been current ones—as the Two Great Commandments and the Golden Rule. Jesus himself according to Matthew called each of these two answers (the basis of) the Law and the Prophets. But when Jesus sticks to his own line, answering or not answering as he pleases, he shows his independence.

There has been much debate as to whether Jesus' teaching is original in the sense of novel. Something has been said of that question in a previous chapter. Far more important is independence, since not newness but selection is its hall mark. There is every evidence that Jesus respected the old and had no cult of novelty for its own sake. As few liberal ministers recall in selecting sermon texts, there is a saying of Jesus in Luke which reads, "The old is good," or perhaps, "The old is better," while in Matthew the instructed scribe is defined as like a householder who brings forth out of his treasure things new and old.

Neither the Sermon on the Mount nor the Cross on Calvary bears witness so much to the originality of Jesus as to his independence. In fact the cross is the very coefficient of his independence—an independence not just for the sake of being different or inspired by reaction and negativeness on Jesus' part. It was his courageous loyalty to the mature judgment he had achieved. I do not understand it as courted martyrdom, or as grandiose playing of the messianic rôle, or as fanatical suicide. Crucifixion is not the penalty for originality but for independence, and that not necessarily in a large area of difference. "I must go on my way," says Jesus confidently, "today and tomorrow and the day following: for it cannot be that a prophet perish out of Jerusalem."

The difficulty of such independence is no less today. The refusal to take sides may be due to intellectual laziness, physical sloth or moral indifference, or it may be due to an assured confidence in a different hierarchy of values from those which divide nations, classes or churches. Jesus had plenty of invitations to accept bad ends to good means if the story of his threefold temptation has any biographical worth. He knew the misunderstanding of friends as well as the hatred of enemies. Mark's emphasis upon the disciples' failure to understand has a verisimilitude that may not be purely editorial, nor need Jesus' taciturnity about his own mission be without the historic basis of a person who keeps his own counsel.

When every controversial subject round about us invites us to surrender our independence, when we are told that every question has only two sides and that neutrality is even by Jesus' own standard impossible, we still must ask ourselves whether the issue, as others present it, is the main issue for us. We shall be often accused of condoning evil, of reducing white and black to gray, of irresponsibility, of idealism or perfectionism, or of trying to live in an ivory tower. Then maturity such as Jesus achieved is very difficult to maintain. To maintain it may be, however, a greater contribution to society than to have a share in those crusades which, though crowned with outward success and victory, contain in themselves, in their spirit and methods, the seeds of ultimate frustration or worse. If I am not mistaken Jesus' mood often anticipated the mood of Thoreau when he said, "If a man does not keep pace with his companions, perhaps it is because he hears a different drummer. Let him step to the music which he hears however measured or far away."

I have already mentioned certain traits of Jesus' mind that are of a simple arithmetical or quantitative character. His maturity may be illustrated by the way he transcends considerations of literal size. He is not imposed on either by the bigness of things or by the littleness of things. He does not ignore the importance either of small things or of great ones.

The evidence in the gospels for this verdict is sufficient. It is expressed often by the usual picturesque and hyperbolic terms which were characteristic of the culture in which he lived. Every culture has its own distinctive terminology. There is, for example, the common human failing of being critical of small things and ignoring the great ones. It is something like that disease known to the psychiatrists in which all kinds of little things, whether fears and worries of the mind, or aches and twinges of the body, receive undue attention. Here is a printed manifesto of a Society that promotes the observance of the Lord's Day. It fulminates against taking children to the Zoo on Sunday, or riding in trains, or against amateur theatricals with their make-ups when undertaken on that day. Even when entertainments are given for the sake of charity or of service men, if they violate sabbatarian strictness they should be forbidden, for, as these pious people declare, the end does not justify the means. Yet it is perfectly evident that these same people have never lifted their voice against Sunday bombing of enemy children, or against riding through the skies on war missions, or against the camouflaging of military installations on the first day of the week. To such matters they do not apply their sabbatarian taboos and still less their moral criterion that the end does not justify the means.

Such a modern example is not very different from what Jesus found in the religious practices of his day, or what can be found in any day. The Pharisees tithed mint and dill and cumin and left undone the weightier matters of the law. As Jesus put it, they "strain out the gnat and swallow the camel."

The lack of perspective in criticizing others is expressed by another set of good Jewish superlatives when Jesus speaks of beholding the mote that is in thy brother's eye and considering not the beam that is in thy own eye. The very currency of the terms and even of this exact expression in the rabbinic literature indicates that the insight into relative values was not unique to Jesus. The continuing failure to implement the insight remains a challenge to the modern Christian.

There is, however, an exactly opposite kind of emphasis which Jesus also exemplifies. It is the capacity to recognize the importance of little things, what the poet calls

That deep insight which detects
The great things in the small.

Twice he uses in gospel passages that other contemporary superlative, a "grain of mustard seed" (Mark 4:31 and parallels; Matt. 17:20 = Luke 17:6), and the same lesson is intended by the parable of the leaven. To "despise not the day of small things" is quite as important as to recognize the significance of great things and is often a good deal more difficult.

At first sight this alternating emphasis of Jesus seems inconsistent, and there are many other features of contrast in the gospel sayings which raise the same question. Obviously in material uttered on so many different occasions, the replies of Jesus quite naturally would include opposite emphases. Critics of the gospels have loved to point out such contradictions. They are especially earnest in playing off Jesus' own conduct against his teaching. We must admit that we have not evidence enough to guarantee the self-consistency of Jesus. We may even question what consistency ought to be expected of him. Our gospels are not all of a piece. The evangelists differ from each other, and even the material which they use had received the impress of different early Christian interests before it was edited into our present records.

Sometimes the variation is more formal and verbal than actual, as when Jesus is quoted as saying:

He that is not with me is against me (Matt. 12:30 = Lk. 11:23).

and

He that is not against us is for us (Mark 9:40 = Lk. 9:50 you . . . you).

At other times it leaves us with more serious questioning.

Even if we cannot correlate all the sayings of Jesus it is plain that there were kinds of inconsistency to which he was sensitive. Here again is a mark of moral maturity. For morally as well as otherwise men grow up very unevenly. Part of their conduct, therefore, is incongruous with other parts, and they can often best correct the situation by levelling up to their conduct at its highest the retarded areas of their moral practice.

I believe that a large part of Jesus' teaching may be classified as aimed at greater congruity, or at least that among the considerations he appealed to in his advice and criticism was the incongruity of conduct of certain kinds with other aspects of a man's behavior. There are in fact several cases where what is left of the words of Jesus is the illustration by which he states the discrepancy, without our knowing what the illustration applies to. Such are the words about casting pearls before swine, about new wine in old wine skins, or about a new patch on an old garment, or about expecting to pick grapes from thorns or figs from thistles. The illustrations remain. They condemn severely the inappropriate as self-defeating. But under what circumstances or with what inference Jesus used them one cannot now tell.

This emphasis on incongruity is particularly true of his criticism of Pharisaic practices. They oppose helping men on the sabbath, but permit helping animals. They evade duty to parents by a device of tradition. The well-known woes of Jesus include in Luke's version the following:

You cleanse the outside of the cup and of the platter, but your inward part is full of extortion and wickedness.

You tithe mint and rue and every herb, and pass over justice and the love of God.

You are as tombs that appear not, and the men that walk over them know it not.

You load men with burdens grievous to be borne, and you yourselves touch not the burdens with one of your fingers.

You build the tombs of the prophets, and your fathers killed them.

While the passage of Luke nowhere uses the word hypocrite, that is regularly used in Matthew's famous parallel and occurs frequently elsewhere. The word deserves some consideration especially in the light of its

history and its gospel context.[1] The English translitera-
tion is probably not a very accurate translation of
ὑποκριτής. Nowhere does any secular writer seem to apply
the Greek word to feigned righteousness, nor does that
meaning fit the gospel passages generally. These seem to
point, as I have suggested, to the incongruity of behavior,
straining out the gnat and swallowing the camel, concerned for the mote and ignoring the beam, rather than
at conscious insincerity. It is difficult to know now what
Aramaic word if any lies behind the Greek ὑποκριτής. The
Hebrew word (*ḥaneph*) so translated in the Old Testament means profane. Neither this nor the literal Greek
meaning of "actor," that is, stage player, fits the gospel
occurrences any better than does hypocrite in English.
To judge from the full contents of the passage is more satisfactory than to trust in the obscure epithet, and the
context implies inconsistency rather than insincerity.
Probably the persons so censured were deceiving themselves more than they deceived others. Matthew uses
repeatedly the adjective blind: "You blind guides . . .
you fools and blind men . . . you blind men . . . you
blind guides . . . thou blind Pharisee." Hypocrisy in
our modern sense is a rather refined evil. It is the homage
which vice pays to virtue. Mere discrepancy is a more pervasive evil, a blindness of sincere men that is curable and
worth trying to cure. With all his love of paradox in
speech, Jesus seems quite out of love with discrepancy in
action.

That some of the behavior criticized is hypocritical in
the modern sense need not be denied. The rabbinic

[1] Cf. A. Lukyn Williams, *Talmudic Judaism and Christianity*, 1933,
Appendix.

sources themselves show sensitiveness to insincerity in their group. Especially the passages where Jesus criticizes fasting, prayer and almsgiving done to be seen of men might be so understood. Yet even here Jesus' concern is not with the public that such acts deceive, but with the ostentatious doer of piety himself whose wrong motive deprives him of the advantages of less demonstrative action. So in another passage he speaks of those who devour widows' houses and for a pretense make long prayers. These shall receive greater condemnation.

The tragedy of such incongruous behavior is recognized by Jesus. He believes others will see the incongruity when it is called to their attention. They are not blind to other, less conspicuous and less important matters. He is not claiming special revelation for himself, or special learning. The wise and prudent have no advantage here over ordinary folk. Good judgment and common sense and a willingness to be aware of what is plainly incongruous and foolish are all that is needed. Jesus has no special theory of epistemology and no doubt of men's capacity to do what is best when they see it. All this has at least negative bearing on his own moral maturity. That was natural, unsophisticated, automatic.

Before leaving the subject we may ask the question, even if we cannot answer it: How Jesus got that way. Modern biography loves to inquire why men became what they were. In the case of Jesus the genetic processes are particularly obscure. The science of form criticism has in my judgment finally dashed our hope for arranging the events of his ministry in any reliable sequence of time. In any case one suspects that the formative influences on his character belong to a time before his public ministry began. It is probably a true instinct, or a valid generalization, which leads Luke in his character- istic summary to say that the child Jesus grew and became strong and filled with wisdom, or that he advanced in wisdom and age and in favor with God and men. Except for the word wisdom these summaries are parallel to those given in the Bible for other children, Samson, Samuel or John the Baptist. Luke also has the story of Jesus' pre- cociousness when at the age of twelve "the doctors" in the temple were surprised at his "intelligence and his answers." It is his wisdom as well as his mighty works that astonish and "offend" his fellow townsfolk on a later occasion.

Wisdom is not a word that has played much part in modern studies of Jesus' character. Perhaps it sounds too patronizing. It did not, in the sense of ethical maturity, play much part in early thought about Jesus either. For that reason we must rely on general considerations, rather than accept or reject what the evangelists were attempt- ing to underscore. Though Matthew evidently is attempt- ing especially in the Sermon on the Mount to contrast Jesus' teaching with that of the scribes and so concludes with the sentence, "The multitudes were astonished at his teaching: for he taught them as one having authority and not as their scribes" (7:28–29), there is reason to believe that originally, in Mark 1:22 (cf. 1:27) the noteworthy thing expressed in that sentence about Jesus' teaching was the miracles which accompanied it.

The sources of Jesus' insight are, some of them, fairly obvious. He knew the Old Testament, but he knew it selectively—as all men know their Bibles. Obviously he

knew the prophets as well as the Law. That he was i
many respects more in line with the prophets may hav
been due to personal temperament, as well as to person⁻
experience. One suspects that he had reacted agains
much contemporary legalism. Probably this was in part
due to a cumulation of experiences, of interviews and
discussions.

But he also knew post-canonical Judaism from the inside. Since our sources for it are nearly all later than Jesus
we cannot assert dependence, but I know of no objection
to the hypothesis of dependence. As already mentioned
the questions asked Jesus were not new questions and
there were no new answers. To choose his answers, not
for fear or favor, was to be as independent as one could be.

In his excellent posthumous volume, *The Theological
Method of Jesus* (The Beacon Press, 1938), the late
W. W. Fenn has dealt with the question of the sources
of Jesus' religious insights. Much that he says is applicable to the moral insights as well. We may doubt whether
Jesus was indebted to some determining formula or
made his comments by applying some conscious underlying principle. But he had probably a rich set of in-
cidents besides the few reported and his reactions to the
behavior of individuals are undoubtedly the sources of
what seem like *dicta* made *ex cathedra*.

Even towards Judaism one cannot formulate an attitude on Jesus' part that is simple and clear, and yet that
is the subject where the materials in the gospels are most
abundant and the probabilities of history would make an
adjustment most necessary.

Dean Fenn thinks the parables are more than illustrations fetched by Jesus to explain points in his teaching.

He thinks they represent the process by which Jesus himself reached his conclusions:

Truth appeared in his mind in the form in which he taught it. Now, as we consider the form of his teaching, we are instantly impressed by its homeliness. There is nothing weird or uncanny about it, nothing unwholesome or strange. When we read his words, we feel ourselves on the familiar ground of common life. There is nothing to indicate that the speaker was dwelling in a different world from ours. Here are the fields and flowers, the growing corn and the nesting birds, the ordinary processes of nature and habits of men. As there is nothing unearthly about his teaching, so there is nothing conventional about it. He is not using borrowed illustrations or customary forms of presentation—all of his teaching has the air of fresh and vivid personal insight, the mark of utter sincerity, in Carlyle's use of the word. If it be true, then, that Jesus learned as he taught, the suggestion would be that through his communion with God, his eyes were opened to divine meanings in common things. This is so significant for our purpose that it will profit us to look at the teachings of Jesus more closely from this point of view. We must keep this idea in mind, in order that we may see whether or not it is really true that the materials of his thought seem to have been derived from his experience with nature and with man.

One thing more impresses anyone who takes the gospels as they stand. Jesus seems ready for each occasion and seems to deal with it as someone well prepared. This is of course natural in stories told long afterward. Hesitation, doubt, inadequate improvisation would hardly have continued to color the report had they existed at the start. At this point we must not trust our sources too implicitly. But it is possible that at this point they are also correct.

The temptation of Jesus is often supposed to belong where the gospels put it, early in his ministry. Already, at least as Matthew and Luke relate the dialogue, Jesus is fully prepared. The use of scripture replies to the tempter's suggestions looks artificial. All three of them come one after another from the same one of the scrolls of the Torah, Deuteronomy. Yet it is characteristic of the maturer piety that the scriptures are already at its command, not so much like Vergilian lots for random decisions or as extraneous authorities, but as embodying the individual's own deliberate judgment and as providing him with convenient formulation of what he has learned.

The story closes with what we may call, if we like, another temptation at Gethsemane and Golgotha. I suppose no one can take such events in his stride. If Jesus prayed to escape "this cup" and even cried as reported, "My God, my God, why hast thou forsaken me?" that was human. It too had its merits for the writer of Hebrews, according to whom precisely such prayers and supplications with strong crying and tears were among the significant formative factors. Though he was a Son, yet he learned obedience by the things which he suffered. This writer does not hesitate to apply to Jesus the common Greek word play παθεῖν, μαθεῖν. He learned from what he experienced. The result was one perfected (τελειωθείς), that is τέλειος, mature.

Yet at Gethsemane one has not so much the feeling that Jesus at last rises to his full height. He has long foreseen the possibility of a violent death, and what is more important he has settled it long in advance that for him the choice is to be God's will and not his own. He is merely doing what is to be expected of him, and what he has been doing all along. He illustrates here his own teaching, "He that is faithful in a little will be faithful also in much."

How far Jesus recognized the process of achieving his own maturity, and how far he could therefore recommend the same process to others is hard for us to know. I would not claim support from Matthew's wording of the commandment, "Ye therefore shall be perfect." But I think we have some hint of his commending to others the same kind of maturity which he himself showed in his advice against worry about food and clothing and particularly in the words about the disciples' behavior when brought before courts of trial. In Mark (13:11), whom Matthew (10:19–20) nearly follows, it runs:

And when they lead you to judgment, and deliver you up, be not anxious beforehand what ye shall speak; but whatsoever shall be given you in that hour, that speak ye; for it is not ye that speak but the Holy Spirit.

In Luke it occurs twice:

And when they bring you before the synagogues, and the rulers, and the authorities, be not anxious how or what ye shall answer or what ye shall say: for the Holy Spirit shall teach you in that very hour what ye ought to say (12:11).

Settle it therefore in your hearts, not to meditate beforehand how to answer: for I will give you a mouth and wisdom, which all your adversaries shall not be able to withstand or to gainsay (21:14, 15).

I like especially Luke's combination of terms in this passage, "Fix it in your minds not to rehearse in advance." There is a kind of Hibernian paradox here as in that phrase of Paul's, "Be ambitious to be quiet" (1 Thess. 4:11).

Such sentences reflect vividly some of the actual experience of the early Christians. In the community which handed down the gospel sayings they found themselves unexpectedly equipped to meet the crises of conflict and persecution. Such resources they naturally interpreted as incursions of divine inspiration and assistance, though a modern psychologist would perhaps refer them to the reserves of courage and determination within the soul of the mature Christian. The subconscious and the supernatural often look alike. If they were available for the disciple how much more for Jesus. For the disciple is not above his master, but, continues the Lucan passage, every disciple when fitted out shall be like his master. Luke's participle here is not the τέλειος of Matthew nor the τελειωθείς and τελειῶσαι of Hebrews, nor is it the Matthean μαθητευθείς, made a disciple. It implies, however, equipment with the master's qualities, κατηρτισμένος.

We are concerned here with Jesus' achievement. To others that too seemed supernatural, implemented by God or inspired by the Holy Spirit. Yet if his maturity was won the hard way and the normal way it is none the less noteworthy or valuable. Perhaps it is more valuable as an example to us. It would remind us that one cannot really improvise. What seems like improvisation is based on practice and experience. A friend of mine wrote me in a time of stress, "I have discovered that one cannot become a Christian in times like this. One must have been a Christian."

I have always been pleased by a curious feature of Greek grammar. It is a perfect imperative, as if you could command somebody not merely to do something, but to have done something. Thus Jesus says to the storm, not "be thou muzzled," as he said to the demon (Mark 1:25 φιμώθητι), but "be thou having been muzzled" (Mark 4:39 πεφίμωσο). That kind of command seems to be the real counsel of perfection in the teaching of Jesus and one lesson of his own character.

There is actually one such perfect imperative addressed to his disciples: "Let your loins be *already girded* and your lamps alight, and you like men awaiting their master, when he will return from the wedding" (Luke 12:35, 36). The constant emphasis upon being awake, whatever its apocalyptic limitations, is an emphasis on readiness, on alertness, and on reserves. In the familiar parable of the ten virgins, the wise ones had laid in extra supplies on purpose for emergencies. Such teaching is not intended for one person or for one occasion but for all. The servant who is warned and ready will be richly rewarded. "But that servant who knew his master's will but did not prepare or act according to his will shall be beaten with many stripes" (Luke 12:47).

Life, then, has a certain continuity about it. The parable of the wise and foolish virgins illustrates the obvious. The foolish virgins find themselves defeated not by their failure in the emergency but by a situation they have allowed themselves to get into. They do not find it easy to see where the trouble lies. I recall a student who when asked by the teacher why he was late to class replied in the tone of injured innocence, after some reflection, "I think I must have started late." Faults, to use Paul's phrase (Gal. 6:1), overtake us. We are caught by the consequences of the past. By hindsight we can see now how it all developed, but it is too late to hope to extemporize a cure.

Happily, says Jesus, the reverse is also true. The result of the other way of life is precisely these unexpected reserves. There is on the day of judgment apparently as much surprise in being told "Inasmuch as ye did it. . . ." as in being told "Inasmuch as ye did it not. . . ." Special rehearsal or preparation is unnecessary. Like the soil in the parable, life may be described as automatic. Character is a normal fruition from the past whether in the case of the disciple or of Jesus.

Perhaps we have some hint or confirmation as to the basis of Jesus' own knowledge if we inquire how he expected his hearers to know. In other words, what was the principle of his own teaching? What source of knowledge in his hearers did he rely on? Did he regard his function as disclosing new facts, or repeating old ones? Was it factual at all? Did he aim to persuade by reason and knowledge and logic?

When the rôle of Jesus as a teacher is carefully explored and many erroneous notions about it corrected, we will find that the process of Jesus' own knowledge and the process of knowledge expected in his hearers closely match each other.

Although the words used in the gospel—disciple and master—suggest even more exactly in the Greek than in the modern English the words for teacher and pupil, the relationship that existed was not the modern one of imparting and imbibing external knowledge. The informational conception of modern education was perhaps the method of some other teachers in Jesus' time, elementary or rabbinic. If so, Jesus did not teach as the scribes, and the ideal disciple of Jesus was not like the ideal disciple whom the rabbis compared to "a cistern that does not leak."

Jesus did not as a teacher pass on recondite data. Even the word secret in the New Testament means always an open secret—news that is available to all and accessible for them to see for themselves. Knowing depended not on the teacher but much more on the hearer. The teacher's function was merely to elicit or kindle the cognitive process. Though Jesus did not use the Socratic figure of the midwife, he might well have done so, for his stimulating conversations appear to have had that effect. To his disciples was given the chance to know the secrets of the kingdom of God because they could perceive as well as see, they could understand as well as hear.

In spite of some passages in the gospels to the contrary I think he expected his hearers to rely more on themselves than on himself. At least once he says this explicitly, expostulating with them, "Why don't you judge *even of yourselves* what is right?" The evangelists with all their reverence for Jesus never represent him as saying, "Why do you not take it from me?" Perhaps Matthew comes nearest to doing so in his formula, "Ye have heard that it was said to those of old time . . . but I say unto you." No doubt Matthew thought Jesus a supreme teacher, and here the evangelist was definitely contrasting his words with the Law of Moses. Hence six times in one chapter he has not only λέγω ὑμῖν but the pronoun ἐγώ. Matthew has a tendency to formulas and stereotyped phrases. Probably both the form and the phrasing of this passage are due to this evangelist as the exponent of a counter-legalism. Certainly the simple, "Ye have heard that it was said" is a poor contrast to an emphatic "I."

The teaching is quite as much to be contrasted as the teacher, and the emphasis may well be placed upon its content, whether it seems as in some cases to extend the Law or whether as in other cases it contradicts the Law. The passages should perhaps be read so that the *but* gives accent to the contrasting ideas: not, an eye for an eye, *but* resist not the evil; not, thou shall not murder, *but* thou shalt not be angry; not, thou shalt hate thine enemy, *but* love your enemies. In the single parallel in Luke to any of these six passages the pronoun is omitted, and everywhere else in the gospels including eight cases in Matthew's sermon on the Mount and some forty beside in Matthew's gospel, no ἐγώ occurs with the words "I say to you," or "Verily I say to you," and the emphasis is upon the content of the following assertion. The single exception is the controversial passage, "and *I* say to thee, thou art Peter," etc. These facts in the synoptic gospels and the contrasting egoism of the teaching of Jesus in the Gospel of John are enough to make us look elsewhere for Jesus' concept of the basis of his pupils' response than in the authority of an *ipse dixi*.

There is much in the gospels as they stand to suggest that the kind of knowledge Jesus looked for was not so much imparted information as insight achieved. There is in fact reason to suppose that he did not refer so often to what his followers were to be told as to what they were to recognize and to discover. The verb *know* means apparently just this when it is used, and may very well have been relatively infrequent on Jesus' lips in the usual epistemological sense.

There is of course the Johannine use of it, found also in a famous synoptic *logion,* with a divine person as an object, but otherwise it is relatively rare in the gospels. Some of the few cases, and of these the last three are of doubtful textual authenticity, are the following:

To Jerusalem—Would that thou hadst known the things that belong to thy peace . . . Thou knewest not the time of thy visitation.

To James and John—You know not what you ask.

To his unbelieving contemporaries—You hypocrites, you know how to diagnose the appearance of earth and sky, why do you not know how to diagnose this time?

To James and John again—You know not what spirit you are of.

Of his executioners—They know not what they do.

To the Pharisees and Sadducees—You know how to interpret the appearance of the sky but you cannot interpret the signs of the times.

These it will be noticed are all negative. Jesus' complaint is that men do not recognize the implications of their attitudes. But this is not something you can simply tell them. It requires understanding, perception, or insight. Positively expressed, it is an acquired experience, like that needed in understanding nature, and once again Luke uses the phrase "of yourselves."

Behold the fig tree and all the trees; when they now shoot forth ye see it and know of your own selves that the summer is now nigh.

In this passage Mark and Matthew use the still rarer word "learn." That verb occurs again in any of these gospels only twice, in Matthew.

Mature knowledge in this sense cannot come from exterior authority, not even from miracles. It depends much more on the inner capacity for response, and Jesus was aware how often that necessary response was lacking. What he says about unintelligence, hardening or blinding of heart, indicates that among his hearers, including even his own disciples, he often found it so. Their advantages and opportunities, so much greater than those that some of their predecessors had enjoyed, were no guarantee of their right response. The road to knowledge was not greater or clearer signs, not more authoritative pronouncements. Such could only affect those who had eyes to see and hearts to understand. Whether Jesus shared Paul's predestinarianism or not, the fact was that men were rejecting reasonable evidence and were bound to do so because of an inner defect.

I often ponder, and especially at Easter time, the closing words of the parable of Dives and Lazarus. As in most paragraphs of the gospels the real point of the parable is probably in the closing words. The dialogue between the rich man and Abraham across the gulf in Hades runs like this:

Dives: I beg you, father, to send Lazarus to my father's house, for I have four brothers, so that he may warn them, lest they also come unto this place of torment.

Abraham: They have Moses and the prophets; let them hear them.

Dives: No, father Abraham, but if some one goes to them from the dead, they will repent.

Abraham: If they do not hear Moses and the prophets, neither will they be convinced if some one should rise from the dead.

How extraordinary that the church with its emphasis on Jesus' resurrection could let these words remain. Perhaps even for the church the evidential value of the resurrection was not as great as it seems to students of Christian beginnings, and possibly it would have been less important still to Jesus himself. It was not really a new factor, nor was Jesus himself a new factor. Men can be tested by what they already have, and if they do not respond to that, they will not respond to miracle or sign, not even to the sign of the Son of Man.

We are far removed here from any contrast between Jesus' authority and the authority of the past. Instead of an emphatic "but I say unto you," Jesus is saying emphatically that it was already said to those of old. Men do not need new teachers but a different inner response. There is no new body of information to impart, there is no new educational technique. Men who habitually do not respond to what was long available can hardly be expected to react any differently now. As elsewhere, we see here that almost mathematical sense of equivalence in Jesus' mind.

The particular motive to which Dives hopes his brothers will respond is fear—fear, of course, with the alternative expectation of positive bliss, or at least escape from disaster. That is an old motive. Moses and the prophets had used it too. They had coupled their demands on men with threats enough, and with promises. Nothing is added by repeating the threat, even if it could be made more vivid and realistic by an eyewitness from Hades. Men who had not responded before will not respond now, at least not unless their springs of action change in kind rather than in degree. To appeal from a lesser fear to a greater one is futile in trying to change them. If the moral teachings of Jesus' predecessors awakened no response, he hardly expected his own to do so. His appeal must be not by imposing miracle or unprecedented threat. He would remain in the line of the prophets. He had no sign but that of Jonah and he admitted that Jonah found proportionately a greater welcome in pagan Nineveh than Jesus was finding in the Jewish towns of Galilee.

How thoroughly appropriate these considerations are to the state of the world today! I constantly hear men expressing hope, I cannot say confidence, in a new and vivid great fear. They have seen devastated cities in Europe or Asia, and they point out as men who have looked across to where Dives was in torment, what lies in store for us unless we repent and reform. They expect us to abjure our international sins out of fright, since we have never done it for higher motives. There is nothing new in their warning.

I have gone a little afield in speaking thus of the motives on which Jesus relied, or did not rely; for I expect to say more on this point in my next chapter. What concerns us here is the sources of knowledge rather than the springs of action which he depended on in others. They appear to be truth, moral truth, recognized as such by the sensitive soul without any very rigid set of external criteria or authoritative standards. They are experience reasonably interpreted. Jesus appeals to the hearer's powers of moral appreciation and response.

Possibly his own grounds of knowledge were the same. Like Dives' brothers, he had Moses and the prophets, but unlike them, he had improved his opportunities and was therefore able to respond to further truth. The secret of any knowledge he had was his disciplined soul, and he expected no more of others than he expected of himself.

When therefore we speak of revelation in connection with Christ, whether of what he knew himself or what he imparted to others, we are to think of the two processes as parallel—a parallelism which the Fourth Gospel loves to dwell on.

Jesus neither receives nor gives ideas. "Revelation," writes John Baillie, "essentially consists not in the communication of truths about God but in the self-revelation of the divine Personality, the truths about Him being abstracted by ourselves from the concrete reality with which we thus become acquainted." [2] William Temple also says: "If God chiefly follows the way of introducing ideas, then revelation itself can be formulated in propositions which are indubitably true. But if he chiefly follows the way of guiding external events, these constitute the primary vehicle of the revelation; and events cannot be fully formulated in propositions; the event is always richer than any description of it." [3]

Leaving technical jargon to one side, the layman will understand if I have suggested that for Jesus the cognitive process was largely recognition. There is a fine respect for the pupil's freedom, a fine confidence in his capacities to know the highest when he sees it. Such a teacher does not overpower or even try to coerce. He may not succeed; but his responsibility is not for success. Probably Jesus did not succeed. Those whom he often wished to gather, as a hen gathers her brood, refused. But no one had co-

---

[2] *Our Knowledge of God,* 1939, p. 175.
[3] *Revelation,* ed. by John Baillie and Hugh Martin 1937, p. 100 f.

erced him. What he learned he learned himself. He voluntarily obeyed. Even a son's obedience can be an acquired knowledge from experience (Heb. 5:8). He humbled himself and became obedient (Phil. 2:8). Such holy obedience is at least what two early Christian writers ascribed him.

CHAPTER VI

BY WHAT AUTHORITY?

Beside the things which Jesus seems to emphasize, we shall do well to consider those beliefs and habits of thought which he takes for granted. A man's assumptions are often more significant of his character, more determinative of his career. Assumptions far more than articulate ideologies cause persons to differ and to quarrel. Both parties are usually entirely unaware of these circumstances. Unexposed or unconscious assumptions on Jesus' part may well have been the cause of the misunderstanding between Jesus and his critics in his lifetime, as they may exist on both sides between Jesus and his critics today. Even his admirers, both then and now, need not be supposed to fathom or to share his underlying presuppositions. Yet these presuppositions are essential elements in his character without which he will not be fully understood.

Especially the modern man needs to be reminded of the gulf that separates his thinking from the mind of Jesus. Jesus was probably much more casual, more naive, more simple in his mentality than many of his modern analysts make out. We can recommend as a beginning of orientation a study of Jewish thinking as we can reconstruct it from the available sources. Psychologically speaking, Jesus probably had much more in common with the

Jews of his time in spite of their mutual recriminations than with the Christians of our time who so lavishly praise him.

Jesus evidently took for granted and could take for granted in his hearers the current Jewish world view. He could count on a belief in God, on a belief in the possibility of man's knowing God's will, and on a sense of responsibility for doing that will. While his attitude to the Law of Moses must have been different in some respects from that of his strictest contemporaries, it was not a fundamental denial of this basic standard of Judaism. He often relies on the Law in argument and undoubtedly he practised many of its non-ethical requirements like the wearing of a fringe on his garment. At any rate, we have no evidence of his having to argue that there is a god or that man can know his will. Though he mentions in a parable a judge who feared not God nor regarded man, we do not find him dealing in actual life with such indifference or atheism. The persons he condemns are not frivolous, but people who, whatever their faults, at least took religion seriously. Sometimes, one is tempted to envy Jesus because he could count on a community that felt a deep sense of duty. His attention could be devoted to helping them discriminate as to what forms of responsibility deserved their support. Evidently in this he encountered difficulties enough.

Just as Jesus could take for granted what theological students are taught to call theism, ethical monotheism, revealed religion and legalism, so he and his hearers had in common a number of assumptions about the future—the coming of a Messiah, the day of judgment, and the resurrection at least of the righteous. There was less explicitness in these beliefs as the nature of the case made inevitable, and there was at least one important group, the Sadducees, who questioned the idea of the resurrection altogether. Jesus' conversation upon this subject with them is therefore almost unique. We have also the puzzling dialogue as to whether the Messiah was the son of David. Otherwise, the gospels suggest that kingdom of God, Son of Man, end of the age, the age to come, were concepts which Jesus could use without defining them, just as he could use Father, Holy Spirit, the Law, or the will of God as part of the religious currency of his people.

Jesus also could take for granted certain moral standards. Among these were naturally those in the ten commandments. He needed only to say that the remarriage of divorced persons was the equivalent of adultery, or that anger was the equivalent of murder. He did not need to reassert or analyze the guiltiness of adultery and murder. That was an accepted datum.

There are other standards which perhaps are in the same axiomatic position. This may be inferred from the fact that they are not even mentioned. Jesus' reported sayings include no criticism of aggressive violence. He seems to condemn rather retaliation and revenge; that is, he is concerned with the way such violence is met. In the parable of the Good Samaritan, not a word is said against the robbers; attention is focussed upon those who did or did not give aid to their victim. Probably Jesus took for granted the censure of aggression and unprovoked violence. In this he may seem to agree with the modern world, but there is a difference, since the latter takes as fully justifiable self-defense, or defense of the innocent, an assumption which the teaching of Jesus challenges.

Conversely, the modern world often attempts to secure reform by the prevention of aggression and violence rather than by inculcating in men the emphasis of Jesus.

The same observation may be made with regard to justice and mercy. It is the latter on which the gospels quote Jesus. Shall we assume that Jesus took for granted the praise of justice, if not its practice, and wished to press upon his hearers the claims of the higher virtue of mercy and forgiveness?

Another observation is here in place. Jesus' concern is with only one side of a social relation, at least with only one side at a time. He deals with the welfare of the rich rather than with that of the poor, with the giver of charity rather than with the recipient; and conversely, in the matter of injuries, he seems more concerned for the recipient and his conduct than for the wrongdoer. The Jewish scholar, Montefiore, who compares him with the rabbis, notes again and again that the rabbis in contrast are concerned with both sides.[1] It is not so clear that here Jesus takes for granted what he fails to mention. His silence may indicate a negative assumption, his preoccupation with one aspect of a social problem.

This fits also another striking silence of Jesus. That is the absence of any reference in his teaching to the altruistic motive. The gospels, so far as they represent Jesus as appealing to motive at all, are, to our way of thinking, exceedingly utilitarian in their sanctions. Jesus freely reminds men of the rewards that virtue will bring, both in this age and in the next, to the man who practises it. The deserts or the welfare of the other party hardly figures

[1] C. G. Montefiore, *Rabbinic Literature and Gospel Teachings*, 1930, pp. 51, 52, 113, 135, 285.

at all in the words attributed to him. I have been told that though Jesus never mentions the benefits to others of our doing what he says, yet he takes for granted that his hearers are conscious of such benefits to others and that he is therefore simply reinforcing their natural altruism by pointing to these self-regarding considerations. This seems to me a quite gratuitous assumption. If this assumption is wrong then we are left with the opposite presupposition that Jesus believed that men would best respond to arguments of self-interest.

Without repeating what I have written elsewhere [2] on this subject let me call attention to a passage in the Gospel of Luke which combines most curiously the references to others and to oneself. After the saying:

If therefore ye have not been faithful in the unrighteous
    mammon
Who will commit to your trust the true riches?

this saying follows:

And if ye have not been faithful in that which belongs to
    others
Who will give you that which is your own?

The sequence here is quite unexpected. Faithfulness in others' affairs is recommended as a prerequisite to a chance to handle our own. To us this is anti-climax. We naturally put it the other way round:

If ye have not been faithful in that which is your own
Who will give you that which is another's?

[2] *The Peril of Modernizing Jesus,* pp. 101–110.

The writer of I Timothy speaks our language when he enumerates among the qualifications of a bishop or a deacon that he be "one that ruleth well his own house," adding, "But if a man knoweth not how to rule his own house, how shall he take care of the church of God?"

The saying of Jesus, if the critical text is to be trusted,[3] implies that fidelity in others' affairs is relatively easy and unimportant. Parallel to the true wealth, which can be entrusted only to those who have been tested and proved, is a man's own interest. We must first make good in our social responsibilities before we can expect our own spiritual treasure.

Experience gives a good deal of evidence to confirm this rather paradoxical sequence. I may appeal to those who find social service the road to personal growth, being willing to attempt to help others without waiting until they are perfect themselves, and in general to the experience so well illustrated in the history of the Old Testament prophets. By identifying themselves with the public issues of their day—the problems of economic justice and of international politics—they achieved such insights as we associate with Isaiah and Jeremiah. The former learned in contrast with the military might of Egypt the significance of God as a spiritual force. The latter was likewise, so far as we know, the first to feel, through his duty to protest a futile war policy of his nation, some of the personal character of religion expressed in his so-called "Confessions."

But our present concern is Jesus' sequence that puts first another's welfare because it means that the last and

3 Some manuscripts at Luke 16:12 read for "your" the similar "our," some read "mine."

best is our own. Thou shalt love thy neighbor *as thyself*.
Even the golden rule implies that our own advantage is
not merely the test but the result of what we do for others.
That advantage is God's gift. So at least I understand the
passives and the impersonal "they" of such sentences:

With what measure ye meet it shall be measured to you again.
Good measure, pressed down, shaken together, running over,
    shall they give into your bosom.

Make to yourselves friends by means of the mammon of un-
    righteousness
That when it shall fail, they may receive you into the eternal
    tabernacles.

The "they" in these passages is, I think, a reverent equivalent for God.

On what sanctions did Jesus rely in his direct teaching
on conduct? It is evident still in our gospels that much
of his teaching was advice to his hearers. He was asking
of them definite actions or attitudes. Probably this was
even more frequent in the original form and content of
his words. Sometimes, quite casually, sometimes in response to direct questions or immediate situations, his
counsel was asked and was given. His teaching was not
systematic, it was not something offered in the abstract.
It was immediate and relevant and concrete.

If that is the case, we are justified in asking, Why should
he expect his hearers to heed it when it concerned them
personally? Of course, when he spoke to one group about
others, the consent of the first would cost them little, but
when, as in most parts of the Sermon on the Mount, he

seems to be giving direct advice, often radical in its requirements, what was there to recommend it to them? It is all very well to say to a man, "Sell all that thou hast and follow me," to others, "Don't be anxious about food and clothing," to another, "From him that takes away thy cloak withhold not thy coat."

Perhaps it is unfair to assume that Jesus himself considered this question. His advice may have been often spontaneous, unsought as well as sought, and offered without much reflection as to how he should make it palatable or effective. Sooner or later, he could not fail to realize that it was unpalatable to many. Certainly it was often without effect. While Levi the publican followed him, the rich young ruler did not. We are rarely told whether interlocutors accepted or rejected his advice, since the evangelists are mainly interested to tell what that advice was. The preservation of his sayings in the First Century and the lip-service they receive in the Twentieth is no evidence that they succeeded in persuading the persons to whom they were addressed. Jesus on more than one occasion is reported as distinguishing those that hear and do, and those that hear and do not.[4] He also was aware of those who call him Lord and do not do the things which he says. This is the important division, and it is to this I think the phrase applies, "He that hath ears to hear let him hear," rather than to any distinction between those who do or do not understand what they hear. Of course from one angle, the response or the enlightenment of men was not in their own control. God can reveal to babes what is hidden from the wise and prudent. Many kings and wise men of the past had

4 Matt. 7:24-27 = Luke 6:47-49; Mark 4:13-20; cf. Luke 8:21; 11:28.

desired in vain to see and hear what Jesus' disciples receive. The disciples are permitted to know the secrets of the kingdom while those outside see and hear without perceiving or understanding. But this is neither the natural nor the prevailing temper of the homely, practical exhortations of the gospels, especially since we think of them as given by a serious teacher to a serious inquirer.

The gospels represent a good deal of this advice as uttered broadcast. This I suppose was the habit of those Christians who repeated it and who combined with it their own urgent message *about* Jesus. Probably we cannot now know how far the teaching of Jesus was offered in the first instance wholesale, sown at random to take root where it could. Possibly some of his words as preserved will seem to us better adapted for such use than others, but their later use may have transformed them from personal and occasional comments to general teachings. The second person singular *seems* more personal than the second person plural and the latter than the third person. It is probable that the material in the gospels has been changed in the direction of both these less personal forms. As the gospels anticipated, what was once whispered in the ear was later proclaimed upon the housetops.

If we may think of a more limited original audience, the ground of Jesus' appeal is easier to understand. A rich man doesn't run to him with a formulated question without some prior conditioning or "build-up." Jesus had a reputation already. Where it was unfavorable, the questioner may well have tried merely to test or catch him, but where it was favorable, there was preparation for an effective answer. Such a dialogue is represented in

Mark 12. A scribe recognized that Jesus had answered other questions well and asks him which is the great commandment. He accepts Jesus' selection with approval, and Jesus, when he saw that the scribe answered discreetly, said to him, "Thou art not far from the kingdom of God."

The gospels also suggest for Jesus a more permanent audience—his disciples. However later motives may have distorted their rôle in the story, the general fact of his having some habitual associates can hardly be questioned. There is the parallel of contemporary Jewish teachers with disciples, there is the survival after his death of such a nucleus. These persons again constitute an audience whose receptivity of Jesus' teaching would be quite different from that of the casual listener, just because they were customary listeners to him. The extent and character of their special susceptibility is imagined in various ways in the usual thought of Christians. It would be influenced by many considerations other than the cumulative acceptability of the sayings they heard from him. What he did and what he seemed to be could give to his words a value that in themselves they could scarcely claim.

The miracles of Jesus are of course one kind of sanction for his words. I am prepared to believe that both Jesus, his friends and his enemies credited him with "mighty works" and that these made both Jesus and his friends take his words more seriously. What his enemies did about the miracles is not so clear. They may have attributed them to magic, but their view does not here concern us. Jesus' teaching gained prestige from his miracles. There can be little doubt of that. These are the two features of his career that loom largest in all the gospels, no matter how differently the several writers apportion them, how differently they weigh them. We have here a transfer of authority from miracle to word. Whatever fallacy modern logicians find in such transfer was not recognized by those ancient persons whose springs of action were involved. If the words on worry or wealth were more heeded because it was believed the speaker cured the lepers and the lame, that is understandable if not defensible. Possibly Jesus himself appealed to such reasons. "Believe me for the works' sake" is the way the Fourth Gospel puts such an appeal. There are hints of the same kind in the synoptic gospels.

In the same way claims for a special rôle of Jesus would provide authority for his teachings. It has done so from a very early time. How early and what rôle are the questions that need to be answered here. I must confess I do not know the answers. When and if his hearers thought him a prophet or *the* Prophet or the Messiah and were known by him to hold such an estimate, both they and he would find again special sanction in his teaching. Possibly the process was ultimately this. Miracles suggest Messiahship, Messiahship authenticates teaching. If so, that is only the other and more direct transfer from miracles to teaching authority expanded by a middle member. Whether the fallacy of transferred authority remains, the logicians may explain, though the historian must add two points.

There is no evidence that Jesus' contemporaries would limit the power to work miracles to the Messiah. Yet a Messiah without miracles, even a prophet without miracles, may have seemed to them unlikely.

There is no evidence that they expected the Messiah to be specially concerned with interpreting human duty.

"A prophet like one of the old ones" might well talk of what Jesus talked about, but the Messiah, so far as hints are given, was to have been a man of action rather than of words.

At the risk of seeming to leave out the real sanction for Jesus' words, in dismissing thus briefly the authority of his miracles and his identity, let me return to other aspects of the question. Can we discover in the sayings of Jesus themselves any ground of appeal? What instincts or responses in men do these words fit?

We moderns are used to commending actions by their expected results. We say, Do this, and such and such will follow. Why will it follow? How do we know it will follow? The answer is usually based on experience or calculation. Jesus too appeals to results. "If the blind lead the blind both shall fall into the pit." "Be reconciled with thy adversary quickly while thou art with him in the way; lest haply the adversary deliver thee to the judge, and the judge deliver thee to the officer and thou be cast into prison. Verily I say unto thee, Thou shalt by no means come out thence, till thou have paid the last farthing" (Matt. 5:25-26). "Put up again thy sword into its place: for all they that take the sword shall perish with the sword" (Matt. 26:53). Such prudential considerations are familiar to us. In fact, the last saying goes back in Egyptian literature many centuries before Jesus.[5]

There is, however, another kind of consequence than that which is the obvious result of natural causes, or the codification of experience. It is the kind of result which is dependent upon the action of God who rewards those

---

[5] Papyrus Spiegelberg quoted by Maspero, *Les Contes populaires de l'Égypte ancienne,* 4th edition, 1911, p. 259 ff.

who do his will. The distinction is a modern not an ancient one. What Jesus seems to say is, Do thus and so, for God would have you do so, and you can count on him to bless you, whether in this world or in the next. This kind of saying is very abundant.

Give to the poor and thou shalt have treasure in heaven.

If ye forgive, God will forgive you.

With what measure ye mete it shall be measured unto you.

He that humbleth himself shall be exalted.

The beatitudes are of the same kind.

We may well ask, however, not, Are these promises true? but, What process of thought, what assumptions and motives lie behind such sayings? Is the character and conduct recommended because it will be rewarded? Is Jesus sensing and calling attention to the forgotten or unobvious results of what he advises men to do? Or does his thought begin with certain desired ends, perhaps in the thoroughly conventional phrasing of the usual desiderata of his contemporaries—like entering the kingdom, or having eternal life, or seeing God, or having reward in heaven—and continue by pointing out just how those ends may be obtained? Sometimes in our sayings the end is mentioned first. They begin, "He that would save his life . . ." "If thou wouldst be perfect . . ." "He that would be first among you . . ." But the problem is the same with either verbal sequence.

I may express my conjecture on this subject—and any answer is bound to be conjecture. Jesus is laying weight not on the result but on the requirement. That is the thing that impresses him. In contrast often to current standards, even in reaction against the theory or practice of persons or groups in his environment, other standards appeal to him for mention or emphasis. Of the two parts of such *dicta* this is prior in significance and in thought. The mention of the result is secondary. It is added as part of a poetic way of speech; it often completes a couplet. It is therefore a somewhat arbitrary form. Indeed it occurs in several forms. Sometimes it expresses from experience the result:

Every kingdom divided against itself is brought to desolation.

When thy eye is single thy whole body also is full of light.

For the present tense of such sayings the sequel or parallel easily substitutes a future tense, and so at other times the sayings anticipate the normal or desired fulfilment:

Ask and it shall be given you.

Blessed are they that mourn for they shall be comforted.

The sanction clause is also chosen for its paradoxical character:

Everyone that humbleth himself shall be exalted.

Blessed are ye when men persecute you . . . Rejoice and be
    exceeding glad . . .

Sometimes the result is described as parallel or appropriate compensation:

If ye forgive men their trespasses, your heavenly Father will forgive you.

Blessed are the merciful for they shall obtain mercy.

He that denieth me in the presence of men shall be denied in the presence of the angels of God.

These cases often involve an interchange of figurative for literal:

Follow me and I will make you fishers of men.

He that loses his life shall find it.

Sell what thou hast and give to the poor and thou shalt have treasure in heaven.

Finally, in many cases, the promised result is a general or conventional phrase:

He that endureth to the end, the same shall be saved.

Whoever gives you a cup of water . . . he shall not lose his reward.

This do (love God and love thy neighbor) and thou shalt live.

No man, having put his hand to the plow and looking back, is fit for the kingdom of God.

Blessed are the pure in heart, for they shall see God.

If this conjecture is right, it relegates to the formal and the less important and the less original the recompense side of Jesus' sayings.[6] In arguing thus we are not guilty of wishful thinking. To the modern mind any emphasis upon motives of reward is anathema. Personally I am not so sure of this prejudice, and it need not bother us that in the recorded sayings of Jesus there is so little if any appeal to altruism in motive, along with the altruism in action, and so much of what is alternatively called eudaemonism, ultilitarianism, the self-regarding and prudential motive. Yet in admitting or even emphasizing this generally unwelcome and selfish-sounding feature of Jesus' teaching one must honestly add what has just been stated about its secondary aspect when psychologically considered.

For how did Jesus know or suppose he knew the relation between conduct of certain kinds and the recompense? Did it come, as is so often claimed, from special insight into the mind of God in whose hands all that befalls men really rests? Was it that knowing God Jesus could infer what behavior in men would or would not please him? Or was it something more nearly just the reverse? If I may again resort to conjecture I would guess quite emphatically the latter. If there was any inference in the matter I think it was just the opposite of the inference from God's mind to man's duty. Man's duty was probably more nearly what was first given to Jesus. To his sensitive moral perception that which was good had an axiomatic, independent and self-authenticating appeal. He appraised neither good nor evil so much by reference to practical results or to a kind of foresight of

---

6 Cf. A. N. Wilder, *Eschatology and Ethics in the Teaching of Jesus*, 1939, p. 22: "If the Beatitudes are typical we are led then to see that sanctions of reward and penalty are formal and stylistic rather than ultimate."

the day of judgment as by a more immediate verdict. The inference he made was that since such deeds and character were good or bad, any recompense expressing the divine verdict would correspond. That there is such a correspondence was a commonplace of the whole view of the world which Jesus shared with his contemporaries, his predecessors and his followers. Probably they operated and we still operate in much the same way. The Hebrew prophets likewise believed that God had a will for Israel and would bless or punish Israel as it kept that will, but they identified that will with social justice and not with sacrifice, and when they predicted disaster it was because the nation was not practising such justice. The injustice was a known and present fact, the disaster was a future expectation based upon it. No insight into the probable course of political history, no calculating of scientific cycles of drought or locusts, no reading of the stars enabled an Amos to say, "Thus saith the Lord. For three transgressions of Israel or for four I will not turn away the punishment thereof." Amos knew that they sold the righteous for silver and the needy for a pair of shoes, and Amos condemned such actions and believed that God condemned them and would punish whatever he condemned.

This mental process, so natural to all theistic thinking, still leaves our question unanswered. At least it pushes it back another step. How then did Jesus arrive at his moral judgments? If they were not derived from a feeling about their effects were they obtained from reason or logic? As I have indicated before there is a certain element of deduction in the sayings of Jesus, a kind of mathematical logic, though not of the abstruse kind which that term signifies in modern philosophical circles. Yet in the main neither he nor his predecessors, his contemporaries nor his followers, identified God's will with reason. The rabbis had their own way of arguing and it involved certain principles of inference from the wording of scripture, of consistency between the parts of scripture, of concession to practical considerations and plain common sense. Back of these were simple dogmatic assumptions—unchallenged, unsupported, unconscious— and an equally unconscious response to what I can only call good moral insight and good ethical taste.

So also while the teaching of Jesus sometimes indicates that point B logically follows point A, it still leaves point A hanging, assumed, unexplained. Nor do the gospels give us any hint of Jesus' thought in process, maturing by observation, or discussion, or experience. In an earlier series of Shaffer Lectures, Professor Dibelius of Heidelberg, makes an interesting contrast

between the manner of Jesus' teaching and the manner of the great philosophers of Greece. The so-called Socratic method teaches by dialogue. Socrates tried to draw out from the mind of his pupils the thoughts necessary for the discussion; every partner of the discussion has the duty of collaborating in a philosophical sense. Jesus—if the tradition of the Synoptists is reliable—did not discuss any subject in such a way. He proclaimed something, he demanded something, he promised something but without any human intermediation . . . None of his opponents can further the discussion by putting stimulating questions.[7]

Yet there was and is an appeal in Jesus' teaching, an appeal that is independent of any authority claimed for

7 M. Dibelius, *The Sermon on the Mount,* New York, Charles Scribner's Sons, 1940, pp. 37–38.

the speaker, of any sweet reasonableness in its logic, or of any inducements by which it is recommended. It sometimes appeals just in and by itself. As we read the Beatitudes and ask why we assent to the congratulations extended to those who exemplify certain traits, and then remember other sayings in the gospels whose ultimate correctness we must admit, even if not able to claim to have obeyed them, what is it that makes us respond to them? Undoubtedly long Christian tradition plays its part, but those who meet them newly from other traditions concur with some of them at first sight, as did some of the common people of Galilee in his own day, and many Gentiles of the succeeding generations. The apologists felt no need to apologize to philosophers or kings for the ethical teachings of Jesus which they quote. His words have sometimes been more highly and honestly esteemed outside the Christian circles than within them.

The reason is so simple that it is hard to state, so hard to state that it is easily conjured into the mysterious or supernatural. Like any other words the words of Jesus find their ultimate sanction in our own consciences. Of course, our consciences have their history, but whatever that may be they are the judges of thought, the august supreme court of our souls. If they concur we simply say, "We hold these truths to be self-evident." We may use arguments to support or to attack the words of Jesus. The arguments are probably secondary and supplementary. At bottom the response is due to a kind of self-validating character in the teachings themselves.

What God's will is is not stated as though it came from an external authority such that its content is a matter of indifference, but men are trusted and expected to see for themselves what is required of them. The requirements of God are therefore self-accrediting.[8]

Jesus relied upon the sheer validity of his truth and on the native discernment of his hearers. . . . His appeal was finally not to fear, or avidness for safety, but to the assent of the heart. This confidence of Jesus in the persuasive power of the truth and in the ultimate moral discernment of common men seems to have taken precedence with him over other enforcing features. His final plea, all eschatological menace apart, is, "And why even of yourselves judge ye not what is right?" (Lk. 12:57).[9]

We may have seemed already to have minimized the eschatological element in Jesus' teaching by suggesting that the reference to rewards does not, in spite of its frequency, represent the real motive behind his exhortations. It is further to be doubted whether the eschatological outlook affected much the content of his teaching. That content was self-validating rather than deduced. That would mean that it was not even based on considerations of shortness of time, and of the consequent differences in standard between proper actions in an emergency and proper actions in an ongoing society. Jesus' teaching was not therefore an *Interimsethik*.

There is, however, another aspect of apocalyptic which may be mentioned here. We shall not do justice to the manner in which the apocalyptic element figures in Jesus' teaching if we ignore it. Though it may not offer the real motive for Jesus' teaching nor affect greatly the content

[8] R. Bultmann, *Jesus*, Charles Scribner's Sons, 1926, p. 73. Cf. Eng. Trans., *Jesus and the Word*, pp. 76 f.

[9] A. N. Wilder, *Eschatology and Ethics in the Teaching of Jesus*, 1939, p. 126.

of what he advised, it did serve to suffuse the whole situation with an intense urgency, by the sheer pressure of time. Jesus' message like John's may be summarized as "Repent, for the kingdom of God is near." The teaching of his disciples in the account of their mission in the gospels and elsewhere in the New Testament carried the same note of urgency. The kingdom of God is near. Before some have tasted of death, before you cover the cities of Israel, before I drink again of the fruit of the vine, that kingdom of God will have come.

This urgency need have altered neither the motives nor the content of Jesus' ethical teaching. It was calculated, however, by its very sense of crisis to put pressure behind what Jesus said. That is often the case with preaching. Men know well enough what they should do and why they should do it. They accept in principle the right standards but they lack the will to convert the standards into immediate practice. They procrastinate, they are careless and dilatory. Jesus calls them to be awake, to be alert, to be ready. The gospels are full of illustrations to point up this demand, and they carry an almost contagious sense of expectancy. "Religion is on tiptoe." Those passages which have rightly or wrongly been used to argue that Jesus thought the kingdom was already present are intended not so much to decrease as to increase this sense of urgency. John the Baptist and Jesus himself point forward. Their significance is prophetic and proleptic. That is exactly what the verb means in the much quoted saying about Jesus' exorcisms. "If I by the finger (or Spirit) of God cast out demons, then the kingdom of God has come" (ἔφθασεν). The kingdom of God has to that extent anticipated its scheduled arrival.

This apocalyptic urgency fits very well the time in which we live. It is particularly congenial to "crisis" theology. [10] But it is not good authority for that aspect of such theology which enhances the contrast between God's initiative and man's dependence. For Jesus nowhere uses it to belittle man's responsibility. Of course, he does not anywhere talk about men building the kingdom. He knows that God alone has put the times and seasons in his own power, and in his good time will bring the kingdom and will allot places in it as he pleases. It is his kingdom and there is no impairment of the divine sovereignty. But Jesus believes firmly in the dignity and the adequacy of men to do their part. It is not a rôle of passive waiting any more than it is a rôle of taking the kingdom by storm. It requires effort even to wait, to hold out with patience, to keep awake and alert and ready. To be fit for the kingdom requires difficult and costly decisions. We must marshal all the resolve we can muster, we must live with loyalty to certain priorities. We shall have temptations to avoid and daily bread to receive, while we pray for the kingdom to come. The elect must cry to God day and night that he will avenge them speedily. Whether he is as prompt as they desire is doubtful. Sometimes God seems too patient and passive. When the Son of Man really comes will he find faith on the earth? The crisis is a crisis for men. The risk is that they will fail. Perhaps if they realize how near the kingdom is they will make the needed decision now.

In much of this, I have relied on conjecture and perhaps have attributed to Jesus certain traits that seem contradictory. Logic very often would set the problems

---

[10] Hence it is emphasized in R. Bultmann's *Jesus*.

a little differently and would seek a more consistent solution. The problems seem to me more psychological than logical, and things are possible psychologically that are not possible logically. The relation of man's effort and God's effort is one of these baffling theological problems. The rabbis discussed it and tried to safeguard both answers. Psychology characteristically recognizes how more than one emphasis can be in an individual mind. We need not be greatly bothered if Jesus too seems to combine two or more aspects of ethical approach. Precisely this makes his character so difficult to analyze, so full of contrast and superficial contradiction. It may be this too which makes him so far from fanatical or extreme, so natural, so human. He is like all personality, an enigma. These chapters make no pretense of fathoming him. While he may help us understand ourselves and God, he is reported as having said, "No one knows the Son, save the Father."

WHAT MANNER of man was Jesus of Nazareth? Most people attempt to answer this question in terms of what he thought, as expressed in his teaching. Professor Cadbury probes deeper; he tries to find out *how* he thought, to understand the working of his mind, the underlying attitudes, emphases, and presuppositions of his teaching, and to relate these to our present-day modes of thought. He deliberately ignores certain fashionable lines of approach, and some questions that are being asked to-day he puts on one side, in order to explore less frequented and less familiar ground, to inquire into the cast of Jesus' thought, to ask how he knew what he knew and why he urged what he urged – even to discuss his motives and aims. The result is a challenging study that will give fresh insights to those who say, "Sir, we would see Jesus."

6s. 6d. net